"A spell is most powerful, and ten by the person who casts it. *Con* those who are ready to begin writi rituals, or spells, this thoughtful bo~~ok provides everything that is needed,~~ from inspiration to finished product."

—Eileen Holland, author of *Holland's Grimoire of Magickal Correspondences*

"Elizabeth Barrette has succeeded in a very difficult task—writing about writing. The result is a work that will help anyone to write prayers and spells that are clear and beautiful. In fact, the book as a whole is an example of good writing; without a wasted word, it is clear, complete, and concise. I myself learned a lot from it, and any reader will too."

—Ceisiwr Serith, author of *The Pagan Family*

"Elizabeth Barrette has created a delightful primer for refining one of our most powerful tools: words. With wit and humor she shows how to get the best from our magickal writings. With Composing Magic, even those of us who lack talent can become wonderful!"

—Lisa Mc Sherry, author of *Magickal Connections*

"Writing school is open and Professor Barrette stands before the class, magical pen in hand. Like a modern Saraswati, she leads us through brainstorming for a topic, rhyme, meter, poetic form, self-editing, and ritual literature. This primer will be useful to anyone who wants to write an invocation or ritual."

—Barbara Ardinger, Ph.D., author of *Pagan Every Day*

"Elizabeth Barrette has added an invaluable resource to those of us who have spent hours writing (and rewriting, and rewriting, etc.) the verbal portion of a spell or ritual to get it to sound just the right way. In her new book, *Composing Magic*, she offers the intrepid poet an incredible collection of resources for creating magic in meter and rhyme. Overall, this would be an excellent book for someone who already has the tools and the knowledge, but wants to tie the ritual together with just the right words. Words are magic, and *Composing Magic* conveys that thoroughly."

—Lupa, author of *Fang and Fur, Blood and Bone: A Primal Guide to Animal Magic*

"In *Composing Magic*, Elizabeth Barrette guides the reader through the how-tos of composing magickal poetry, ritual, spellcraft, and chant, offering clear instruction and detailed examples. The two chapters on poetry alone are worth the price of the book, and are guaranteed to empower the hidden poet in every reader. This text should find a place in every magickal library, where it is sure to become dog-eared from enthusiastic use."

—Susan "Moonwriter" Pesznecker, author of *Gargoyles*

"An excellent guide for beginning writers of spells, incantations, chants and prayers. Will help a novice break through inhibitions and blocks. A great resource for individuals and groups that breaks down the elements of poetry, prose, and ritual. Suitable for teachers of writing classes as well as individual aspiring writers. A wonderfully practical approach to writing for individuals and groups."

—Ellen Evert Hopman, author of
The Forest Priestess: A Druid Novel

"At last, a writing book specifically for the Pagan writer! *Composing Magic* fills a gaping hole in the crowded 'how to write' category of books. Whether you're a professional Pagan writer, a priest/ess of a large coven or circle, or a solitary practitioner, *Composing Magic* will show you how to write spells that bring results, poetry that sizzles, and rituals that truly honor the God/dess."

—Smoky Trudeau, Writing Coach and Instructor, author of *Cycle Fire:
Poetry that Honors the Seasons of Woman*

"I had great pleasure and satisfaction from reading this book. As far as I know, there is nothing else like it, and the author has done a lasting service for the Pagan and magical communities. In an age when people use tedious, poorly written boilerplate "ritual" text, trivially copied with minor thematic changes from one location to another, Ms. Barrette shows us with considerable skill and wisdom how we may create truly artistic and skillful ceremonial scripts and poetry, and even more, she shows us how to approach magical writing in general. I highly recommend this book, and will be listing it to my own students as essential reading."

—R.J. Stewart, author of *The Merlin Tarot* (*www.rjstewart.net*)

"*Composing Magic* is at once encouraging, educational, and practical. The examples and exercises supplied in each chapter marry technique to intent, giving readers an opportunity to both absorb and create sacred compositions of various kinds. In brief, Barrette's first book is a worthy read and a worthy reference for anyone seeking to add a more personal dimension to Pagan practice."

—C.S. MacCath, author of *Yundah* and
Bringing Woden to the Little Green Men

"Deftly combining experience, insight, and inspiration, Elizabeth Barrette's *Composing Magic* makes writing for ritual a meaningful, spiritual experience in its own right."

—Alex Bledsoe

Composing Magic

How to Create Magical Spells, Rituals, Blessings, Chants, and Prayer

Elizabeth Barrette

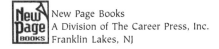

New Page Books
A Division of The Career Press, Inc.
Franklin Lakes, NJ

COMPOSING MAGIC
EDITED BY KARA REYNOLDS
TYPESET BY MICHAEL FITZGIBBON
Cover design by Leeza Hernandez/Conker Tree
Printed in the U.S.A. by Book-mart Press

To order this title, please call toll-free 1-800-CAREER-1 (NJ and Canada: 201-848-0310) to order using VISA or MasterCard, or for further information on books from Career Press.

The Career Press, Inc., 3 Tice Road, PO Box 687,
Franklin Lakes, NJ 07417
www.careerpress.com
www.newpagebooks.com

Library of Congress Cataloging-in-Publication Data

Barrette, Elizabeth.

Composing magic : how to create magical spells, rituals, blessings, chants, and prayers / by Elizabeth Barrette.

p. cm.

Includes bibliographical references and index.

ISBN-13: 978-156414-935-0

ISBN-10: 1-56414-935-8

    1. Witchcraft. 2. Magic. 3. Charms. 4. Ritual. I. Title.

BF1566.B267 2007

133.4'4--dc22

2007007236

Dedication

This book is dedicated to all the folks, including but not limited to those listed here, in approximate chronological order, whose contributions have influenced my writing in more ways than I can count:

To my divine patrons, for gifts, guidance, and inspiration.

To my grandparents and my parents, with love and gratitude, for years of reading aloud and storytelling, and sundry other encouragement in the adoration of lore and language.

To all the writers whose works I've read, and to the bards of old—I'm standing on the shoulders of giants. Wow, what a view.

To the handful of classmates in junior high and high school who read the results while I developed my poetic craft by writing a poem almost every day.

To all the good writing teachers I've had, for demonstrating what to do; and to all the *bad* writing teachers I've had, for demonstrating what *not* to do.

To Professor U. Milo Kaufmann, for introducing me—*on the very day we met*—to a colleague as "Elizabeth Barrette, future famous writer," and for priceless instruction in the arts and skills of poetry, literature, revision, faith, and teaching. I hope I live up to your expectations.

To my partner Doug, with love and gratitude, for unparalleled assistance in polishing both the book and its author.

To all the editors whose comments have improved my writing; and especially to Anne Newkirk Niven, who taught me much of my editing skills.

To my fans, who have been pestering me for a book long since; may you enjoy it as much as I've enjoyed your appreciation of my work.

To Suzette Haden Elgin, for teaching me somewhat about the science of language and its artistic applications.

To M.C.A. Hogarth, for companionship, illumination, and applause. When reaching for the stars, it's nice to have someone neck-and-neck on the quest.

To all my friends who have provided encouragement and patience along the way, and in some cases input on things that wound up in these pages.

To the students and faculty at the Grey School of Wizardry, whose enthusiasm for the Bardic Arts helped convince me that this book is a needful and welcome thing.

And to all those not specifically mentioned, who by word or deed touched my life in ways that have bettered my craft and my book.

Thank you. I'll try to pay it forward.

Acknowledgements

I extend my thanks first to Oberon Zell-Ravenheart, for getting my foot in the door so this book could manifest, and for writing the foreword. I also thank Susan Pesznecker and C. Rainbow Wolf for contributing sample compositions.

Contents

Foreword:
Magic Words

by Oberon Zell-Ravenheart

Magic exists in many forms. There is Natural Magic, which is the magic of all the living world around us: the magic of the changing seasons, of birth, life, death, and rebirth; the magic of stones and stars, plants and planets; the magic of the great spiral dance of cosmic creation and emergent evolution, from the double-helical DNA molecule to the double spiral of great swirling galaxies.

Earth, Air, Fire, Water—each have their particular Elemental magics, intrinsic to their respective Natures. And each with their blessings and their furies: fertile soils and shattering earthquakes, cozy hearthfires and erupting volcanoes, cleansing rains and devastating deluges, gentle breezes and raging hurricanes.

There is the magic of sacred places, usually associated with myths, deities, and spirits: storm-riven mountaintops, haunted ruins, burning deserts, tidal seashores, ancient temples, deep forests, crystal caverns, sparkling springs, circles of stones. High places, low places, and in-between places.

All these are magics that we *experience,* and that mages and sages of all magical traditions seek to understand and harmonize with. The single most important teaching of Wizardry is: "Everything is alive; everything is interconnected."

And yet, there is another kind of magic altogether—the magic that we *do*. These are the magics that arise from every act of conscious intention; magics of our own design, choice,

9

and creation. And these magics manifest through our unique ability to translate our experiential and imaginal worlds—both inner and outer—into the symbol forms of language. These are the magics of words.

It is said that Adam, the first man in Jewish tradition, was given the assignment by God to name all the animals in the Garden of Eden. This is what we do as humans—we name things. Perhaps the strongest motivator for explorers and scientists to make novel discoveries is that whoever finds or creates a new thing gets to name it—often immortalizing themselves with the appellation. In magic, the Law of Names states that "Knowing the name, you know that which is named; knowing the complete and true name of an object, being or process gives one complete control over it. What's in a name? Everything!" (P.E.I. Bonewits).

In all traditions and cultures throughout the world, magic words are used in rites and rituals, circles and ceremonies, songs and celebrations. "To bind the spell every time, let the spell be spake in rhyme," says the Wiccan Rede. Chants, invocations, incantations, poems, and prayers call in the deities, raise power, direct energy, bestow blessings, heal hearts, transform lives, commune with the gods, and excite a sense of wonder in those who hear, as well as those who speak. It is important for modern mages to learn how to create and present these words within a magical and spiritual context.

The Magical Law of Words of Power confirms that: "Certain words are able to alter the internal and external realities of those uttering them, and their power may rest in the very sounds as much as in their meanings. A word to the wise is sufficient" (P.E.I. Bonewits).

Magical words play many roles in ritual, which may include poetry, prose, or a combination of both. Writers choose from diverse literary tricks to make their compositions evocative. This book presents different types of magical writing, from short chants to complete rituals. Historically poets, bards, and skalds—specialists of many names and lands—served their people by memorizing and reciting vast repertoires of lore. Today, cultural exchange includes everything from writing books to enacting public rituals at Pagan events.

Humans are storytellers, and we live within our stories. Thus, we are all as much mythical personages as we are creatures of flesh and blood. We each create and live out our own personal mythology as we grow, learn, travel, and share our lives and our dreams with others. Wizards in particular understand the magical importance of stories and myths, and we seize the power to tell the stories in an intentional way that shapes our collective reality—telling us who we are, where we came from, and where we are going.

It is said that a man is as good as his word. The most powerful Wizards and magicians have always been superb wordsmiths—poets and storytellers, bards and balladeers, lyricists and novelists, speakers and writers. With the power of words, a true Wizard can hold an audience "spellbound," foment a revolution, topple tyrants, exalt the worthy, and create the future by instilling (or awakening) mythic archetypes. Do not underestimate the power of words to transform the world; indeed, there is none greater! As Edgar O'Shaughnessy says in "Ode":

> One man with a dream, at pleasure,
> Shall go forth and conquer a crown;
> And three with a new song's measure
> Can trample an empire down.

Elizabeth Barrette is a renowned and skilled magical wordsmith, and a deeply respected modern Wizard who contributed exquisite poetry and insightful articles for my *Companion for the Apprentice Wizard,* as well as *Green Egg* magazine, which I published through three decades. It has been my pleasure to work with her on various cooperative endeavors through the years, such as the dictionary and boilerplate projects, in which a number of Pagan leaders formulated updated entries for dictionary and encyclopedia definitions pertinent to our practice, and composed standard-ized responses to general media inquiries.

Elizabeth is an award-winning poet with the true bardic gift. In our work together, I have oft times requested of her an appropriate piece of poetry for some magical purpose or other. Usually she is back to me within hours with something that is so elegant that anything else would be unimaginable. The first time she did this I was reminded of the legendary Doreen Valiente, who was praised by Gerald Gardner for having the same ability, and with whom I believe Elizabeth may be aptly compared in inspiration and eloquence.

Known to thousands of readers as the managing editor of today's foremost Pagan journal, *PanGaia,* Elizabeth is also the dean of studies at the online Grey School of Wizardry, where she reviews and edits to perfection every class that is taught in the school. A professor of several departments, she devel-oped and teaches a full course on composing ritual poetry for all purposes and occasions, some of which is included in this book.

Although many books and articles have provided notable examples of word magic, few have attempted to explain and instruct how to actually create it. And certainly no one else has done so as effectively and in such depth as Elizabeth. She has that rarest of gifts—the ability not only to execute her craft as a master, but also to teach it to novices and appren-tices. It is a privilege to sit at her feet and learn from her. And I look forward to experiencing the fruits of her teachings in improved rituals, chants, poetry, and songs to reverberate throughout the worldwide magical community. For this work is not only *about* "Composing Magic"; it is itself a brilliant magical composition!

—Oberon Zell-Ravenheart
Headmaster, Grey School of Wizardry
www.GreySchool.com
Winter Solstice, 2006

Preface:
What You Will Find
in This Book

You hold in your hands a guide to magical and spiritual writing. *Composing Magic* explains how to create simple and complex works, from poems and prayers to spells and rituals. Designing your own compositions gives them more power and meaning for you. You don't need to be an experienced writer to get satisfying results.

What you do need is a basic familiarity with common Pagan ideas and practices. This book offers a way for intermediate and experienced practitioners to expand their skills and knowledge. I have made an effort to explain processes and vocabulary that might be new to some readers, but no single text can cover everything. So, this isn't a suitable "first" book for novices; for that you need something similar to *The Spiral Dance* by Starhawk or *People of the Earth: The New Pagans Speak Out* by Ellen Evert Hopman and Lawrence Bond. If you've already read a book or two about Paganism, and performed or attended a few rituals, then you have enough of a foundation to start writing your own materials.

If you are not Pagan, but intrigued by magical and spiritual writing in general, you can still find much useful information here. The processes of writing and connecting with divinity remain similar, though the details may vary. Just seek examples from your own tradition that match the categories in the text. That said, welcome to the exciting world of mystical writing.

Chapter One:
The Basics

There is more to magic words than "abracadabra" and "hocus pocus!" There is more, even, than "please" and "thank you." Words are the medium in which we think, exchange, and preserve our ideas. Sharing words means touching souls—sometimes, changing minds. The right words can lift a heavy heart, bring hope, revive a dream, even draw down the moon to a circle of worshippers. Life is breath, and words are breath given meaning. What could be more magical than that?

In some cases, the power is in the sound; certain terms work almost as a password, granting access to a pool of energy or to mystic knowledge. Names have a similar effect, which is why they are so often kept secret, with titles or kennings—metaphors for magical items or deities—used instead. In other cases, the shape of written words provides the power, such as the triangular "abracadabra" charm, or sight rhymes in poetry. Some ancient prayers and incantations retain their original power, but it is often lost if they become too well-known. Power can even be stolen—or stolen back—with a word, as in the checkered history of "witch." Most of the time however, the magic lies in the meaning rather than the words themselves. The words merely point to the ideas the speaker invokes. What else can the power of words accomplish?

In magical practice, words are tools, as much as the objects on your altar. Words can part barriers and sever bindings, like an athame, and likewise they should be honed to a perfect edge. Words can direct and focus energy, like a wand, and likewise they should be chosen with care to make their point. Words can receive and contain power, like a chalice, and likewise they should be watertight so that nothing leaks out and nothing can breach their wall. Words can ground and stabilize things, like a stone, and likewise they should be solid and weighty. Words can evoke protection and invoke the divine, like a pentacle, and likewise they should weave together in a flawless pattern. Words are your tools. Are you ready to learn how to use them well?

When you think of witches, wizards, and other magical figures of myth and history, they tend to stand out as wise people whose words have an immediate effect on what happens. This holds true whether they are casting a spell, writing a magical inscription, or speaking to other people. Their words shape reality. Now consider some of the magical people you may have met in real life. Chances are, you can recall a powerful ritual, a glorious song, or a sublime blessing. Maybe what comes to mind is a workshop or other presentation in which the speaker held you enchanted for an hour or more. But how did they do all those marvelous things?

The power of such achievements lies not just in individual words and phrases, but primarily in larger pieces such as poems, chants, prayers, and rituals. Magical composition is the art of laying out words in a deliberate pattern to achieve a specific purpose, similar to laying out magical tools on an altar to cast a spell. It's among the most useful abilities for a practitioner to have, because personalized magic is more potent than something generic. Magical composition is what allows practitioners to come up with exactly the right material for the occasion at hand. So how did they learn it?

They learned by practice and study. Some of them had teachers, and others learned on their own through reading and experimentation. These are things you can learn to do too.

This book explains how to plan and create spells, blessings, and other works. It describes what magical composition is, how it works, and what you can do with it. Written samples give you a chance to read and analyze what other people have done, and exercises at the end of every chapter encourage you to try new techniques—practice is the best way to improve your skills. Before long, you too will be wielding the power of magic words with confidence!

Bards of Old—and New

Throughout history, people especially skilled with the magic of words have held prominent positions in many different cultures. All religions, of course, have their own clergy: Priests and priestesses customarily handle prayers, blessings, and spiritual ceremonies. Wizards and other magical practitioners may cast spells and work mystical rituals. But there are always a few special people who draw their power *from* words—who compose the poetry, the chants, the legends, and the magical songs, passing them along to others as well.

The Greek tradition of rhapsodes dates back to classical antiquity. Clad in their distinctive traveling cloaks (which remain visible on some Greek artifacts), they journeyed from town to town, reciting the educational verses of Hesiod, the epics of Homer, and the satires of Archilochus, among others. Their influence on the sacred pageantry of ancient Greece still echoes in modern rituals of the grand, formal, public sort. Another symbol associated with rhapsodes is the wand, representing their right to speak before an audience.

The Celts were famous for their bards, who thrived from ancient times well into the medieval period.[1] They composed poems in honor of their royal patrons and eulogies on the death of lords and heroes. They also devised piercing satires of wicked or miserly people. It was said that a bard's song could charm birds and beasts, sometimes even the weather. People welcomed them because they carried news and messages too. Bards carried a gold or silver branch as a symbol of their authority. The bards, Ovates, and Druids formed three branches of the educated populace. Although the Druids in particular were persecuted, the bards survived longer, bequeathing a tradition of Scottish, Welsh, and Irish harpers that continues to this day.

During medieval times, Scandinavia and Iceland had skalds. These great warrior-poets traveled from country to country as the guests—and sometimes counselors—of kings. They composed and transmitted the Old Norse legends and poetry, particularly the Eddas. Many of their poems were originally magical. Their songs, stories, memorials, and testimonials recorded battles, marriages, and other historic occasions. They were especially known for their kennings. Knowledge of the kennings was an important sign of mystical education. Much of what we know of Viking culture comes down from the skalds, and their material still appears in some college classes.[2]

In West Africa, there live the Griots. These storytellers specialize in the history, genealogy, and oral tradition of a specific village or an important family. They are poets, singers, and musicians belonging to a special caste and clan of their own, rarely marrying outside it. In most West African societies, only a Griot may perform the duties of a Griot; such things are forbidden to other people. Although the height of their service has passed, oral tradition being challenged as more people become literate, there are still Griots in some parts of Africa today.[3]

So the roots of magical and spiritual writing run deep. The lines between song and spell, poem and prayer, theater and ritual, and even myth and history, are not always sharply defined. The traditions of word magic are ancient and widespread, and they continue to influence the modern world.

What we think of as "contemporary Pagan culture" dates back several decades—a mere sliver of time compared to that occupied by our predecessors. Yet although the forms and context may have changed, the basic concepts have not. By whatever name, the bards of today serve much the same purpose as in the past. We still hail our heroes, mock the arrogant, beseech the divine, praise the beautiful, and coax the world to shape itself according to our will. We still teach our children with story and rhyme. The drummer who leads the chanting around the fire circle, the priestess who orchestrates the main ritual, the poet whose verses appear in print, the guitarist who sings of gods and goddesses, the Pagan radio host, the Webwizard designing a coven home page: These are our modern bards.

Times change, and we change with them. To the old we have added whole new options: public festivals and open rituals with attendees from all over the globe; Pagan magazines, novels, and nonfiction books; recordings of songs, chants, meditations, and more; radio, television, and movies; even the Internet. And that's the way it has always been, for the craft of bards—old and new, by this name or any other—depends on taking all the threads handed down from past masters and weaving them into a tapestry of words meaningful to the present audience. (You can especially see this process in movies, given the Hollywood fixation on remakes and sequels.)

This is the tradition you join when you take up magical composition. Feel free to draw from it, add to it, or even play with it. Your predecessors certainly did.

The Essentials of Magical Composition

Literature appears in all mystical and spiritual traditions, around the world, and throughout time. Whether in text or oral tradition, magical composition frames the core ideas of a system so that they can be shared. People use poetry to stir the spirit, and spells to improve their lives. They use chants to raise and direct energy. They use rituals to celebrate the seasons, mark turning points in their lives, and recount myths and legends in sacred theatre.

This book focuses mainly on spellcraft and spirituality of the eclectic Pagan sort, but remember that you can use the same techniques in other contexts as well. Magical composition adapts to any system or situation. Likewise, the spoken and written word are simply two different aspects of the same thing. Composing magic does not necessarily mean writing it down—for example, chants are often created spontaneously, out loud—but writing it down offers a convenient form of long-term storage. The basic process of composition remains the same, no matter which magical or spiritual tradition you belong to, whether you compose by speaking out loud, writing, or typing. Experiment to see what works best for you.

There are three basic applications of magical composition. The first is personal use. You can keep it strictly for yourself, using your work only in solitary spells or ceremonies. Poetry works well as a mnemonic device for making facts easier to recall. Prayers are always heard by the one(s) to whom they are addressed, even if not spoken aloud; so you don't necessarily have to be alone to be "private" in application.

The second is semi-private use. This covers small rituals held with family or friends. With just a few familiar faces, stage fright poses much less of a threat, and a good writer is a treasure for any ceremonial group lucky enough to have one. Many folks never go farther than this to share their magical composition, and that's fine.

The third is public use, and here things get a bit more complicated, because there are many ways to make your writing "public." You might publish it in magical magazines or other venues. You could incorporate a blessing into a large ceremony at a festival, or design an open ritual held for public enlightenment and enjoyment. You may record songs, chants, or poetry on CDs, cassette tapes, or other formats.

No matter what format you choose, or what use you intend for your work, all three applications derive from one source. The process of magical composition remains the same for all. First you decide what you want to create, next you do background preparation, then you write a rough draft, and finally you polish it. Chapter Two presents these steps in detail; subsequent chapters explain how to apply them to different types of magical composition.

Although the process of composition and presentation can feel rather nerve-wracking for some folks, sharing your work with an audience holds great rewards. First, you honor your muse and your divine patrons by using your gifts, which encourages them to give you even more. Second, audience interaction and feedback can help you hone your skills. Applause feels good, and you may gain respect as your reputation grows. Finally, if you discover a true talent for magical composition, you may sell some of your work, win writing contests, or get invited to an event as a guest of honor. None of these things will happen if you write only in your secret Book of Shadows, so dare to share.

Don't Panic, This Is Easier Than It Looks!

Magical composition need not be brilliant to be effective, especially in private or semi-private applications. Let me emphasize this: You *do not* have to write like Starhawk or Walt Whitman in order to create effective rituals, spells, and magical poetry. It's nice if you *can,* but it's not essential. Don't put a stop to your writing before you start, just because you don't feel that you can measure up.

Worth mentioning is that very few people have *all* the qualities of a great writer and performer, especially not at a universally high level of development. Most are skilled at some things and not so skilled at others. The legendary writers and performers tend to excel in one or several areas to the point that nobody notices the stuff they do less well. This book will help you figure out your strengths and emphasize those, while downplaying your weaknesses.

You should always write to the best of your ability. You and the universe know what that is, at any given time, so to do less is insulting to both. Whatever your best is, that's good enough. Most professional fiction authors wholly or mainly aim at entertainment, which makes technical quality crucial; but in our case, it's the function we care about the most. A fancy aluminum watering can may look nicer, but a wooden bucket will still get the job done. So it is with magical composition: A competently written, heartfelt blessing will serve the purpose, and indeed is likely to work better than a brilliantly written but halfhearted one.

Here we focus on relatively short pieces of magical composition, less daunting than a whole novel or nonfiction book. The shortest of these items, such as chants, may run only a few lines; a complete ritual usually fills several pages. They are also more active than ordinary literature—you cast a spell to alter reality, chant to raise power, and so forth. Therefore, such magical compositions are more often performed aloud rather than read silently off a page.

Because the ear can be more forgiving than the eye—and because a performance gets people caught up in the cadence— you can get away with things such as near rhymes and extra syllables in a poem or song, as long as the result *sounds good.* Repetition in text seems dull, but in a story or ceremony it helps people feel secure; they know some of what's coming, without spoiling the climactic moments. Think of how things come in threes in a European fairytale, or in fours in Native American legends; the same pattern tends to hold true in rituals for each of those cultures. Conversely, some people learn better by reading than by listening; in that case writing down a song, blessing, or other piece of magical composition can make it easier for you to share your work and keep track of what you're creating.

You may worry that you "don't have the talent" for magical composition. Talent is an innate ability, particularly a creative or artistic aptitude. However, it does no good unless developed, and it makes up only part of the equation. The other part is skill: the ability to use knowledge effectively, which is an *acquired* aptitude. Talent is something you're born with, as much a gift as a sprinter's speed or a musician's perfect pitch. Skill is something you develop yourself, similar to a musician's repertoire of tunes. Talent without skill won't get very far, for lack of direction. Skill without talent can accomplish a fair amount, because some tasks simply aren't very demanding; and skill with even a little talent can accomplish a lot. You can find ways of using one to compensate for lack of the other throughout this book.

Many aspects of magical composition relate to skill, and thus can be taught and learned. Theory, for instance, explains what makes a piece of writing work and why it works—or why it doesn't work, if it's a bad example. We've just covered a little of that and will get into more in later chapters. Writing techniques are the "tools" of composition. They include such things as rhyme, meter, alliteration, imagery, symbolism, word choice, and organization. These usually come with specific definitions and examples. It's possible to create a technically flawless ritual that has no punch to it whatsoever, just as it's possible to create a technically imperfect ritual that raises tremendous power. However, it is much easier to create a powerful ritual if you understand the tools and theory of ritual design! If you can read, and you're willing to put in some practice time, then you can learn to write effective rituals, chants, spells, and other magical material.

Research skills are also important. They bring you the raw materials you need. Books, magazines, the Internet, and other people are just a few of the resources to explore. Read ancient myths, look up examples of good rituals, study poetic forms, compare symbolism in different traditions, and so forth. Collect photos or drawings of things that seem sacred or magical to you; these make excellent inspiration when you run out of ideas. Careful research can make your material more accurate and more vivid.

Other aspects of magical composition, however, appear to be innate. If you have them, you can hone them to their full potential—but if you don't happen to have them, you can learn to work around that. One of these is the eye for what would make a fresh, interesting topic. Writers tend to look at the world a bit differently than other people. Do your best to cultivate an appreciation for the unexpected and the unusual; they inspire some of the most memorable writing. If you don't find ideas popping into your head spontaneously, then you can compensate by using other resources for inspiration, such as myths or seasonal changes.

Then there is the voice. Bards, priests, and priestesses all tend to have a commanding verbal presence. When they speak or sing, they captivate the audience with the quality of their tone and enunciation. They can give forth great beauty and power. Some singers and poets are blessed with a voice for engrossing performances. Other people have an ordinary voice but a perfect sense of *timing*, which is valuable for leading chants and rounds. Whatever voice you have been blessed with, practice will improve it for use in a magical context. This is an excellent way of sharing your compositions with other people.

All of these things get thorough attention in the chapters to follow. You will discover the process of writing, its tools and techniques, magical poetry and its many forms, the crafting of spells and chants, how to attract divine attention with prayers and blessings, the parts of a ritual and how to assemble them, and ways in which you can share your work with other people. Ideally, you should work through the chapters in order, because they build on each other to some extent. But it's okay to skip ahead if you need to compose something specific, such as a blessing, and you haven't gotten that far yet. When you reach the end of each chapter, do the exercises thoughtfully and save your work so that you can observe your progress. It is also useful to go back and repeat some earlier exercises, choosing a new topic—this is a good way to get yourself moving again if you get stuck, or to measure your comparative progress.

The most important thing to remember in composing magic—as in all things—is to trust your instincts. You know your native language. You know what topics matter enough to you that you want to cast spells for them, pray over them, or celebrate them in rituals. Just follow your heart, and you won't go wrong.

Exercises

Use the following exercises to explore the concepts presented in this chapter. You may do all of them, or just the ones that appeal to you. It's a good idea to revisit these after you've read later chapters on specific types of writing, and combine them with other exercises.

Exercise #1: Reading Examples

Read at least six examples of magical composition, of at least three different types, from any source. Spellbooks, poetry anthologies, prayer books, and magical Websites are all good choices. As you read, think about the items you've chosen. Which do you like the best, and which the least? Why?

Exercise #2: Memorization

Memorize a brief sample of prose that appeals to you, at least a paragraph long, and not more than one page. Find something that would be convenient to know by heart, something you can actually use—such as an excerpt from "The Charge of the Goddess," or a favorite prayer. How difficult or easy was it to memorize? Would you rather memorize material or read it off a page?

Exercise #3: Your Journal

While studying magical composition, keep a journal or Book of Shadows, and save your thoughts and exercises. Write in it frequently, and it will give you a record of your progress. Start by choosing one piece of mystical literature and writing about what it means to you. What makes this item stand out in your mind? How did you first encounter it? How would you consider using it in a ritual? Which are your favorite words and phrases? Subsequent exercises will suggest more things to put in your journal.

Exercise #4: Magical Words

Everybody knows some "magic words" (the aforementioned abracadabra and hocus pocus, plus alakazam, presto-chango, and sim sala bim, to name a few). Many of these have become so public and commonplace that they have lost a lot of their power. Yet they still conjure up thoughts of magic whenever you hear them. Research your favorite magic word to find out where it came from and what it really means. Write a spell, a poem, or a blessing using its history as inspiration.

Exercise #5: Historic Figures

Consider all the storytellers, singers, poets, clergy, and performers who have gone before. Whom do you most admire? Whom would you like to be if you could? How do you think they worked their magic? How are they similar to, and different from, their counterparts today? Imagine yourself as such a historic person, and describe in your journal what a day in that life would be like.

Chapter Two:
The Writing Process

Many people find the process of writing to be mysterious. They have a hard time figuring out exactly how to go about it. Although always a bit magical, creativity need not remain opaque. You can learn to write effective magical compositions. As with most things, the solution lies in breaking a large, complicated process into small, manageable pieces.

This chapter explores the different stages of writing:

I. Planning
  A. Brainstorming
    1. Listing
    2. Freewriting
    3. Looping
    4. Spidergram
    5. Collage
  B. Research
II. Preparation
  A. Preparing the Body
  B. Preparing the Mind
  C. Preparing the Situation
III. Composition
IV. Revision
  A. Seeking Feedback
  B. The Finish Line

Follow these steps if you aren't sure how to get started, if you get stuck, or if you feel overwhelmed. Of course, you can also just jump right in and start writing. Different methods work better for different writers. The detailed descriptions here should help you figure out what you prefer.

Planning

Begin by considering your goal. Magical composition is a means to an end. Thus, before you can write anything, you must decide what you want to accomplish. Are you charging a magical artifact in ritual space? Working with a familiar, in the flesh or in spirit? Casting a spell to improve your memory when you study? Warding your room to keep out negative thoughts? Your objective should shape the form, tone, and content of your writing. As much as possible, write what excites you. Your enthusiasm will spread to your audience.

The form refers to the organization of specfic types of writing within a broad category of purpose. For example, a ritual to enhance memory would benefit from rhymed, metered poetry, with the structure of the verse serving to enhance recollection. A ritual involving a ferret familiar would do better with prose or free verse, matching the chaotic nature of ferrets. The tone refers to the mood or atmosphere the composition creates, such as an emotional effect or a flavor of magic. A warding ritual should sound fairly serious in tone, with an emphasis on positive expressions to block out negativity. Charging a new windchime for your Air altar, however, calls for a lighthearted and playful tone. The content is what the composition is all about. In each of the previous cases, the writer's objective sets the subject of the content—the memory, the ferret, the wards, the windchime, and so forth. These may subdivide into separate parts; for example, working with a new ferret might include both bestowing a magical name and consecrating her as a familiar.

Time and space constraints also influence what you write. How long a piece do you need? A brief blessing takes less time and energy to produce than a complete set of Quarter calls and dismissals. When do you need the final draft? If your high priestess asks you to write an invocation to Lugh for Lammas on August 1, don't wait until July 31 to begin; start working on it immediately. Knowing these parameters before you begin keeps your writing on target.

Brainstorming

Use brainstorming techniques to generate possibilities by activating the intuitive rather than the rational part of your mind. These can also get you unstuck if you run into writer's block partway through a project. Select one or more techniques appropriate to the size and style of your project. Numerous options exist; here are a few of the more popular ones, from simple to more complex. We'll use the example of "house blessing" throughout, to show how each technique explores the same topic in different ways.

Listing

The process of writing a list makes you focus on thoroughness.[1] For a house blessing, you might list all the rooms in the new house, and then consider ways to bless each one. List as many colors as you can think of, and describe how each relates to the idea of "home." List the available altar tools, and how you could use them in a blessing. By looking at the less obvious items on a list, you can discover options that might not have occurred to you otherwise.

Freewriting

Write a broad topic ("house blessing") at the top of the page.[2] Set a timer for several minutes. Write continuously, without pausing, without worrying about grammar or spelling. Write down whatever pops into your head. When the timer rings, stop writing. Read over what you wrote and highlight the most interesting words or phrases ("territory," "kitchen witch," "house wards"). Freewriting "breaks the ice" of the blank page, and makes it easier to move into more careful composition.

Looping

To narrow a topic further, pick a term from a previous brainstorming session (such as "house wards" from freewriting) and use it as the subject of another session with the same technique or a new technique.[3]

Spidergram

This map begins with the core topic and branches out into subtopics.[4] First write your subject ("house blessing") in the center of the page and circle it. Next, add some other words related to that subject ("family," "sacred space," and so on). For each of those new words, add several related words (so "sacred space" might lead to "fireplace," "kitchen," and "bedroom"). As clusters of connected words form, circle them to indicate which ones go together. Draw lines to show relationships between the various clusters or individual terms. Try to fill most of the page. The circled subtopics can become sections within a ritual, and individual concepts within the circle could turn into paragraphs or verses. Spidergrams illustrate how things relate to each other, and you can dress them up with color coding, different shapes or line patterns, and so on, to make the connections pop out. See page 44 for a completed spidergram.

Collage

This trick gives visual-minded people a familiar foundation on which to compose.[5] Look through some magazines or catalogs for pictures that relate to your topic. Watch for colors, patterns, body postures, and such, as well as complete scenes. For a house blessing you might select images of gardens, houses, people holding hands, and home-cooked meals. Cut out your favorite pictures and glue them onto cardboard. Refer to your collage for inspiration while writing. An attractive collage also makes a good altar tool for focusing intent during a ritual.

Research

Research expands your knowledge of a topic so that you can write about it more effectively. It may help you decide what to write and how. Use a variety of sources: books, magazines, Websites, and people. Look up your topic—handfastings, money spells, Yule rituals, and so on—and investigate how other people have handled it. Also consult your own previous experience of similar rituals. What have you seen people do that you would like to emulate? What mistakes can you avoid? If possible, consult more experienced people; interviewing a priestess who often leads public rituals can yield valuable information.[6]

For a short project, you may need only a little inspiration before you can sit down and write the piece you want. (Covens often parcel out ritual composition: If you will be calling East at the esbat, you may need to write the opening and closing for that Quarter, and nothing else.) For a long composition, especially a complete ritual, take notes on anything that seems useful. That way, if you need to go back and consult a particular myth or table of correspondences, you'll know where to find it.

Keep your notes in a format that works for you. Some people like to store theirs in a computer file, for easy searching and copying. Others prefer traditional 3 × 5 index cards, convenient for sorting by hand or laying out on the floor. A notebook works well too, especially for large amounts of notes. This isn't a class project, so your notes can be as simple or elaborate, serious or whimsical as you want. Doodle in the margins if it helps you remember an altar layout, hand gesture, or the like. I know an artist who routinely takes notes with illustrations.

Preparation

Now you know what you want to write—a chant, a blessing, an entire ritual—and what you want to write it about. Next, prepare yourself and your materials for writing.

Preparing the Body

Whenever possible, compose magical works when you feel healthy, well-rested, and content. Avoid writing when you feel sick, tired, or upset. Not only does your mood affect your creativity and effectiveness, it leaves an energy imprint on the work itself. Writing in a bad mood can also cause your subconscious to link "writing" with "miserable," which can lead to creative blocks. Gentle stretches reduce the possibility of muscle cramps or stiffness;[7] for this reason some writers do yoga before a long session of writing.

Engage your senses to inspire sense imagery that will pull your audience into your writing. Smell has the strongest effect on memory and state of consciousness. Open a window to enjoy the great outdoors. Burn incense or wear essential oil to boost creativity, such as peppermint, lemon, rose, ginger, neroli, or bergamot. If you always use the same scent when writing, after just a few repetitions, smelling that fragrance will make your brain think, "Ah, it's time to write!" Flavors work much the same way as smells, so many writers like to have a cup of coffee or tea while writing. Others have a favorite type of chewing gum or finger food.

Music or other background sound sets the mood. Try albums of ritual drumming, Pagan songs or chants, and music from ethnic religions. You may find vocal music inspiring or distracting while you write prose; experiment to find out which. Many writers do not listen to music while composing poetry, because the meter of the music can disrupt the meter of the nascent poem. However, if you need to cover up nearby noise pollution, *nonrhythmic* soundtracks can help a lot. Get the kind of "relaxation" album that plays nature sounds without an instrumental overlay. Similarly, running water relaxes and inspires, so consider a tabletop fountain. Match the type of sound to the topic of your writing if possible.

Set the scene with appropriate colors. If you get nervous or tense while writing, surround yourself with something soothing, such as cool colors (blue, green, violet) or earth tones (brown, olive green, brick red). If you get sleepy, use warm colors (red, yellow, orange) or neons (hot pink, highlighter yellow, electric blue).

Likewise, choose objects to keep you engaged. Slowly changing patterns encourage a dreamy or meditative state when you stare at them, good for jostling loose new ideas when you get stuck. A mobile, wind-spinner, or rainbow prism in the window works well for this. Paperweights, crystals, and worry stones keep your fingers busy while you mull over what to write next. Some writers like textured pens or pencils for this purpose as well.

Preparing the Mind

Make a habit of doing things that feed your creative potential. Read the works of other writers, discuss literature with friends, attend cultural events, contemplate paradoxes, spend time alone in introspective places—whatever inspires and refreshes you. These things generate energy, whenever you do them, that you can use then or later to fuel a specific composition.[8]

Invoke any patrons of creativity you wish. Divine, historic, and legendary figures with a connection to writing may lend you their aid. Writers in general, and magical writers in particular, often form a close relationship with their muse. Greek mythology describes nine Muses, each overseeing a different type of creative expression. Writers may also have individual muses—a benevolent spirit or aspect of self that brings inspiration. Many writers develop rituals or habitual actions to invoke their muse(s) when they prepare to write.

Memory paves the way for new experiences and provides excellent inspiration. Think back over some of your favorite rituals and other magical activities, especially those with a similar topic as your intended composition. Aim to convey a similar sense of enchantment in your writing. Many writers begin by rereading a previous project or by revising an earlier section of a work-in-progress before moving on to the next section.

Clear your mind of other concerns and concentrate on the project at hand. Writing requires a focused and receptive state of awareness. For a small project, such as composing a single prayer, you may simply close your eyes and take a few deep breaths. For a large project, such as a set of related pieces like openings/closings or a whole ritual, you may prefer a five-minute meditation.[9]

Preparing the Situation

Work in a place that you find comfortable. Adjust the temperature (indoors) or your clothing (outdoors) so you're not too hot or too cold. A good chair and a level writing surface help, but some writers like to compose in unusual positions— or even while walking around.

Some people need to write in private, because they find interruptions and distractions unbearable. In this case, choose a low-traffic area and turn off phones or other intrusive devices. Other people need to write in public—coffeehouses or libraries make excellent choices—to avoid boredom or brainlock. For Nature compositions, you may wish to write outside. Wear sunblock and insect repellant, or take other necessary precautions for comfort. For fresh inspiration, try writing in an unusual location: sitting in a tree, on a boat, or at a museum.

Of course, if you find the idea of all this planning and preparation too daunting, you *can* simply grab a notebook or a keyboard and start writing. Plenty of writers do so. These steps are recommended because they make it easier for many people to get started, and they tend to improve the quality of the final product.

Composition

Now get out a pencil and paper, or open your word processor. It doesn't matter whether you choose to write by hand or type on a keyboard. Paper is more portable; pencil can be erased if you want to make changes, but pen offers permanence. Use different colors if you want. Computer files are easier to copy or print, and allow different fonts. Remember to save your work frequently if you write using a computer!

Put something on the page right away. If you already have a good idea of what you want to write, then jump in and write it. Otherwise, you can take smaller steps—begin with the title if you've decided on one. List some ideas for things you want to include in the composition. Don't worry too much about spelling, rhyme, or anything fancy for now. Just jot down whatever pops into your head. Use your notes from the planning and preparation phase. Try out different words and phrases. Talk out loud if you like, or sing, or hum; learn what works for you. Listen for expressions that sound exciting and magical. This part of writing is like throwing a lump of wet clay on the potter's wheel: You just need something to get ahold of.

Shape the composition into the structure you have selected. Structure is the arrangement of parts and concepts within a composition. Sort your ideas and phrases into the structure. This part of writing is like squeezing clay into the general bowl shape.

Once you have some basic ideas to work with, write a rough draft. You may start at the beginning and write straight through to the end, developing everything in order. It's okay to work out of sequence, though, putting down lines and paragraphs as they come to you. At this stage, pay attention to grammar and word choice; express yourself as best you can. Remember to use your thesaurus; repeating a word too many times can undercut its power, unless it belongs to a refrain or a chant. (See Chapter Three for more details on using a thesaurus and other reference books.) This part of writing is like coaxing the clay into the smooth curving walls of a bowl.

If you get stuck, do a little more research. Who are the patron deities, ancestor spirits, totem animals, or other helpful powers associated with your goal? What are the colors, directions, Elements, or supporting symbols? You should feel captivated by particular words, sounds, visual descriptions, or additional imagery.

When you finish your rough draft, read through it from beginning to end, checking for completeness and coherence. Did you leave anything out? Are the pieces in the right order, or do you need to move something? Once satisfied with your rough draft, set it aside. Wait a while, depending on length, before you revise your work—the way you would set aside a clay bowl to let it dry. This allows you to see what you actually wrote, instead of what you *meant* to write.

Make sure to save your notes! Also, save early versions of your composition if you set it aside before you have a complete rough draft (which happens frequently with longer works). This way you can study the progression of your work as you do more and more pieces of magical writing.

Revision

After completing the rough draft, polish your work. Revising your composition means finding and fixing a variety of flaws. A short project such as a chant may need only one round of revision; a more complicated project such as a whole ritual may need several rounds. Make sure that every subsequent draft represents the absolute best you can achieve at that point in time.

You may find it helpful to learn some of the common symbols used in editing and critique, a kind of shorthand that indicates what you want to change and how. Most writing handbooks illustrate a long list of such symbols; you'll see several of the most important ones on the sample page (page 44). Online sources, such as Linda Besen's site at the University of Colorado at Boulder, also show editing/proofreading symbols.

During revision, look for large-scale and small-scale problems in your composition.[10] Make sure that the parts are in the right order, that nothing important is missing, and that what you wrote does what you want it to do. Add, delete, or move things if necessary. Also look at your phrasing. Fix any sentence fragments or run-on sentences, reword awkward phrases, and find synonyms for overused words. Finally, check your spelling, grammar, and punctuation; fix any typos.

Seeking Feedback

You may choose to revise your work alone or with assistance. Revising alone retains a certain purity of voice, and protects your privacy, which may win out if you also practice magic alone. However, outside feedback almost always improves the quality of your finished composition. Remember that you are not your composition; critique of your writing is not necessarily criticism of you personally.

Find a friend, covenmate, or someone else you know who is willing to read your writing and give an honest opinion. He or she may give you new ideas or spot flaws that you missed. For most compositions, you only need a single first reader. For a complicated project or something intended for publication, you may want more than one. See Chapter Twelve for further details.

The Finish Line

Finally, write out the finished draft of your composition. Always save a copy of your work, preferably in both electronic and paper formats. Consider memorizing your composition too. Magical writing tends to yield much greater effect when recited than when read off a page.

Exercises

Use the following exercises to practice the writing skills presented in this chapter. You do not need to do all of them; it's okay to pick and choose. However, some of the later exercises use the results from earlier exercises as a starting point, so it's a good idea to read through the whole list before deciding which ones you want to do. You may also find it useful to do some of these exercises more than once; return to them after you have read a couple more chapters, or after a few weeks. Then compare the results with your earlier ones.

Exercise #1: Topics and Types

Choose three topics that you would enjoy writing about, such as abundance, love, a patron deity, or an upcoming holiday. Write them in a row across the top of a page. For each topic, pick three types of magical composition that might suit it, such as a poem, spell, or prayer. Write the types under each topic. Try to use different types of composition for the different topics.

Exercise #2: Ask the Right Questions

Of the topics used in the first exercise, choose two. For each topic, choose one type of magical composition. Answer the following questions for each composition.

- How long a composition do you want to write?
- How much time do you have to finish it?
- Will your composition remain private or be shared with other people?
- How much experience does your intended audience have?
- Do you expect to use this composition inside or outside?
- What materials or tools do you need to perform this composition?

Write a paragraph describing the context of your composition. You may use the lower portion of your previous exercise page for this.

Exercise #3: Brainstorming Practice

Start with a blank page. At the top write a broad topic such as wisdom, herbalism, or elderhood. Set a timer for 3 minutes. Using the topic as a place to start, write continuously until the timer rings. Do not feel compelled to stay "on topic" or worry about spelling, grammar, and so on. After the timer rings, go over your page and highlight interesting words or phrases.

Choose a word or phrase that you just highlighted., and copy it onto a fresh page. Set the timer for 3 minutes and freewrite on the new topic. You may continue looping this exercise as long as it holds your interest.

Exercise #4: Looking Up

Pick a topic from any of the preceding exercises. Look it up in three different resources, such as a book, a magazine, and a Website. Take notes, making at least two entries for each resource. Experiment with sorting your notes into different patterns that you might use for composition.

Exercise #5: Making Sense

Most people have a preferred sensory mode, usually sight or hearing. Which sense do you prefer? What are some ways you could excite this sense while you write? Revisit one of the magical composition ideas that you explored in Exercise #2. Write the composition in a neutral environment. Now add something to stimulate your preferred sensory mode. Write another composition from Exercise #2. Which composition do you like better? Which was easier to write? Why?

Exercise #6: You and Your Muse

Do you have a personal muse? If so, what is your muse like? If not, read about the Greek Muses and pick one of them. Write a paragraph or two about your relationship with the muse.

Exercise #7: Exploring Context

Describe your usual writing circumstances—indoors or outdoors, private or public, quiet or noisy, morning or evening. Change one parameter and write something in a different situation, drawing inspiration from your brainstorming results in Exercise #3. Now return that parameter to your usual, and change a new parameter. Write something else based on your brainstorming. Compare and contrast the two compositions. Do you think you'll write in either of the new situations again, or will you stick with your usual?

Exercise #8: Order and Disorder

Use your notes from Exercise #4. Write a composition, allowing yourself to skip around, jump ahead, double back, whatever takes your fancy. Let the piece evolve as it wants to. Next, repeat Exercise #4 with a whole new topic. Write a composition about the new topic, but this time, begin at the beginning and write straight through to the end. Resist any impulses to go out of order. Which method made more sense to you? Which composition turned out better?

Exercise #9: Writing in Wind and Sand

An ancient type of offering to the gods involved composing something in an impermanent medium, and letting it fade without keeping a copy. Compose a wholly spontaneous paragraph or verse of praise to your favorite deity, ancestor, totem, or other higher power. Write it with a stick in wet sand, or with your finger on a frosty window; or simply speak it aloud. Let it vanish into the world, to be enjoyed by the spirits alone. How do you feel about letting it go?

Exercise #10: A Favor from a Friend

Take a composition that you wrote for a previous exercise. Share it with a friend and ask for feedback.

Which comments did you agree with? Which did you disagree with? Revise your composition using at least some of your friend's suggestions. Do you like the piece more or less this way?

Revision Sample

To celebrate Earth Day, you decide to plant an ash tree with the help of some friends. Some of your fellow volunteers are Pagan, others Pagan-friendly. You've written a rough draft of a blessing to read over the tree, and you want it to sound inclusive of everyone's beliefs. Let's see what happens during revision....

Your Rough Draft

Although we walk different paths, Earth Day stands for what we all have in common. We all call this planet our home, and we must take care that home in order to survive. By planting this ash tree, we affirm our faith in the future. In Norse tradition, the World Tree is a gigantic ash named Ygdrasil. Ygdrasil is home to a giant squirrel and a giant eagle. In Greek mythology, "the race of men" is called "seed of ash." Some Christians believe making an offering an to ash tree on Ash Wednesday will keep away evil spirits. Draw now on those forces to strengthen this young tree. We bless its roots, its leaves, and its trunk. In the name of Odin, in the name of Zeus, in the name of Christ, may this ash grow and flourish!

Your First Revision

Although we walk different paths, Earth Day stands for what we ~~all~~ have in common. We all call this planet our home, and we must take care ^of that home

in order to survive. By planting this ash tree, we affirm our faith in the future. In Norse tradition,

the World Tree is a gigantic ash ~~named~~ Ygdrasil
Ygdrasil is home to a giant squirrel and a giant
eagle. In Greek mythology, ~~"the race of men"~~ is
humanity
called "seed of ash." Some Christians believe
making an offering an to ash tree on Ash
Wednesday will keep away evil spirits. Draw now on
those forces to strengthen this young tree. We

bless its roots, its leaves and its trunk
In the name of Odin, ~~in the name~~ of Zeus, ~~in the name~~ of Christ, may this ash grow and flourish!

In rereading your work, you realize that you left out the word "of" in the second sentence, so you make a note to add that. You make the third sentence more concise by moving "Ygdrasil" after "World Tree" and deleting "named." "The race of men" seems sexist, so you change it to the more inclusive "humanity." The words "an to" are reversed, so you put them in the correct order. You also decide to exchange "leaves" and "trunk," so as to list the tree's parts in order from bottom to top. You delete repetitions of "in the name" to make the last sentence more concise.

This is a clear improvement. However, you think that you could do better, so you ask your friend Chris to provide some feedback as a first reader.

Your First Reader's Suggestions

~~Although we walk different paths,~~ Earth Day
stands for what we have in common. We all call
this planet our home, and we must take care of
that home ~~in order~~ to survive. By planting this ash
~~tree,~~ we affirm our faith in the future. In Norse
Yggdrasil
tradition, the World Tree Ygdrasil is a gigantic ash.

~~Ygdrasil is home to a giant squirrel and a giant eagle. In~~ Greek mythology, ∧humanity ~~is~~
calls
~~called~~ "seed of ash." Some Christians believe making an offering to an ash tree on Ash Wednesday will keep away evil spirits. Draw now on those
∧
positive
forces to strengthen this young tree. We bless its roots, its leaves, and its trunk. By all that we hold sacred, ~~in the name of Odin, of Zeus, of Christ,~~ may this ash grow and flourish!

Chris thinks that the blessing needs tightening. This includes deleting several phrases, and the whole sentence about the World Tree's inhabitants. Chris also points out that you have spelled "Yggdrasil" as "Ygdrasil," and that it would be prudent to specify "positive" forces. The list of specific deities is replaced with something briefer in length and broader in scope.

After reading this critique, you decide to implement most of the changes, except where Chris suggests deleting "tree" after "ash."

Your Final Draft

Earth Day stands for what we have in common. We all call this planet our home, and we must take care of that home to survive. By planting this ash tree, we affirm our faith in the future. In Norse tradition, the World Tree Yggdrasil is a gigantic ash. Greek mythology calls humanity "seed of ash." Some Christians believe making an offering to an ash tree on Ash Wednesday will keep away evil spirits. Draw now on those positive forces to strengthen this young tree. We bless its roots, its leaves, and its trunk. By all that we hold sacred, may this ash grow and flourish!

Useful Symbols

Delete ~~excess~~ excess words.

Insert word between two other words and mark
   a   correction

typos for (corection)

Exchange (things,) words, (phrases) or

rearrange words (easily.) You can also transpose two
words (this) like!

Sample Spidergram

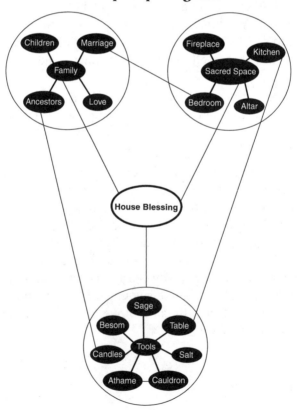

Chapter Three: Writing Tools and Techniques

Writers employ many tools and techniques to create compositions, much the way painters use a variety of brushes, colors, and strokes to create pictures. Most of these tools and techniques apply to multiple types of writing; some are more specialized. In mundane contexts, their purpose is largely artistic, and you probably learned some of this in school. In magical writing, however, all of these things serve to gather or direct energy. Most of these tools and techniques have a rich history in magic and religion, but the reasons and effects are rarely explored in detail. Here we'll explore both the artistic and the mystical uses.

The tools and techniques divide into related clusters:

I. Tools
  A. Writing Supplies
    1. Book of Shadows
    2. Pen of Art
    3. Other Materials
  B. Reference Books
    1. Dictionary
    2. Encyclopedia
    3. Rhyming Dictionary
    4. Thesaurus
    5. Other Books

II. Techniques

  A. Sound Effects

    1. Onomatopoeia

    2. Alliteration

    3. Consonance

    4. Assonance

    5. Rhyme

    6. Rhythm and Meter

  B. Literal Language

    1. Concrete vs. Abstract

    2. Sense Imagery

    3. Parallels (Anaphora)

  C. Figurative Language

    1. Allusion

    2. Epithets

    3. Kennings

    4. Metonymy and Synecdoche

    5. Personification

    6. Simile and Metaphor

    7. Symbolism

    8. Synaesthesia

III. On Balance and Analysis

Tools

Writing involves both tools and techniques. Tools are the physical objects you use to preserve your words. The type of tools you choose can influence what you write and what energy it holds, allowing you to make your compositions more magical. For the most part, though, tools are simply a means to an end, and you can compose without them if necessary.

Writing Supplies

Your writing tools collect power through repeated use, as with any other magical tools. Some people therefore choose to keep their writing implements and materials on their altar, or conversely, to consecrate their writing desk as an altar. You may use one set of tools for all your writing, or keep separate sets for the creative process and the magical application.

Book of Shadows

A Book of Shadows provides an ideal place to keep your magical compositions. This can be a simple spiral-bound notebook, a three-ring binder, a fancy leather-bound journal, or a file on your computer. It should be safe and comfortable to write in—it should be sturdy enough that the cover won't fall off or spit out the pages into a mud puddle, and should not have any sharp corners or protruding wires that could snag clothing or skin. If you're going to leave your Book of Shadows in the house, an ordinary notebook is fine, but if you're going to take it hiking, you need something that can take a beating and still hold together. Decorating the cover (or choosing one already decorated) with symbols of magic or creativity helps cement its purpose. A Book of Shadows shares the symbolism of the chalice, cauldron, and other feminine tools whose purpose is to "contain" something—in this case, words.

Pen of Art

A "Pen of Art" is a general term for a pen (or pencil) dedicated to magical writing. It is most often used to write out spells or sign mystical documents. Although an ordinary ballpoint pen or pencil can serve this purpose, most magical writers prefer to use something fancier: a ballpoint pen topped with an ostrich plume, a natural quill pen, a calligraphy pen, a mechanical pencil with a silver barrel, or the like. (Don't worry if you write messily with a dip pen; it takes practice, and the energy imparted through writing by hand outweighs penmanship in most cases.) A Pen of Art equates most directly to a magic wand, but it also shares the symbolism of the staff, athame, and other masculine tools whose purpose is to direct energy.

Other Materials

Other writing materials may also come in handy. For example, if you've chosen a quill for your Pen of Art, you will need ink to dip it in. Magical inks such as "dove's blood" and "dragon's blood" are available, as are ordinary inks in many colors. Likewise, keep some high-quality papers for writing out the kind of charms that need to be wrapped around something or burned as part of a spell or ritual. If you share your compositions with other people, you'll probably want a computer printer so that you can easily make multiple copies.

Reference Books

A good reference collection is a tremendous asset to any writer. You can supplement this by doing research online or in your local library, but it's much more convenient to have what you need on your own shelves. Although some editions rise above the competition, most reference books within a category are pretty interchangable. If you want a specific title and it's out of print, then search for it in used bookstores, or online through Amazon Books or AbeBooks.

Here are a few of the most important books.

Dictionary

A regular dictionary gives the correct spelling, pronunciation, and meaning of a word. This makes it easier to use unfamiliar words correctly, write metrical poetry smoothly, and read out loud any composition you have written. Get the biggest dictionary you can afford, such as a collegiate or unabriged version; the magical field includes many obscure words, and a larger dictionary will feature more of those than a smaller one. A good choice is *Merriam-Webster's Collegiate Dictionary* (11th Edition).

Specialized dictionaries serve a similar purpose for a more limited subject area. Several magical dictionaries exist, such as *The Watkins Dictionary of Magic* by Nevill Drury. These provide excellent inspiration for topics, and they cover esoteric concepts much more thoroughly than conventional dictionaries.

Encyclopedia

Often a set of volumes rather than a single book, an encyclopedia offers fairly detailed entries on a range of topics. An encyclopedia can be broad in focus, as is the famous *Encyclopedia Britannica*, or much narrower, as is *The Encyclopedia of Witches and Witchcraft* by Rosemary Guiley. A single entry may give you enough information for a complete composition, or you may find yourself following "see also" references through several related entries.

The original paper format of encyclopedias has largely given way to massive online databases. These have the advantage of search engines—but you can't spread them out on your living room floor or idly flip through the pages looking for inspiration. Specialized encyclopedias tend to appear in print format still, usually one to three volumes, and you can easily find general encyclopedias in a used bookstore. Experiment with online and paper encyclopedias to discover which you prefer.

Rhyming Dictionary

This resource evolved especially for poets who work in rhyme. A rhyming dictionary lists all the words that end with a particular sound. Usually this includes one-syllable (aye, by, fly) and two-syllable (bellow, cello, fellow) rhymes, and sometimes also three-syllable rhymes (quivering, shivering). This makes it much easier to find rhymes for a key word in a poem you're writing, or to check the pronunciation if you're not sure whether a rhyme is perfect. Good rhyming dictionaries include *Random House Webster's Pocket Rhyming Dictionary: Second Edition* and the *Oxford Rhyming Dictionary*.

Thesaurus

This reference lists synonyms and antonyms for a given word. Use it to keep your writing from becoming repetitive, especially in longer compositions. *Roget's Thesaurus of English Words and Phrases* is a traditional thesaurus. *The Random House Word Menu* by Stephen Glazier is an alternative thesaurus organized by topic, so that for instance "musical instruments" includes a list of many different types of drums.

Other Books

Additional resources depend largely on your personal interests; the previously mentioned books benefit most magical writers. A book about your own spiritual or magical tradition is an excellent choice. Also, look for books featuring your favorite type of writing. If you want to write prayers and invocations, you may want a guide to deities and their stories, such as *The New Book of Goddesses and Heroines* by Patricia Monaghan or *World Mythology* by Roy Willis. If you plan to write lots of poetry, pick up a guide to the different forms, such as *The Book of Forms: A Handbook of Poetics* by Lewis Tresco. For ritual design, turn to books similar to *Rites of Worship: A Neopagan Approach* by Isaac Bonewits.

Of course, you don't have to buy a whole shelf full of reference books at once. Start with one or two books that you expect to use frequently, such as a dictionary or a mythology guide. Then gradually expand to more specialized books, such as a rhyming dictionary if you write poems. You can often find reference books at a used bookstore. Online resources can substitute for paper references too.

Techniques

Writers can choose from a vast assortment of word tricks to make their writing effective and entertaining. Some of these help distinguish poetry from prose, and others appear in both. The choice and use of techniques gives each writer a unique voice, so study them with care.

The language in which you write—because if you know more than one, you should practice writing in all of them—also influences your choices. For example, the Celtic languages lend themselves to incredibly intricate forms that rely on repeated sounds. Good Chinese writing includes appropriate quotations from famous historic sources such as the *Tao Te Ching*. Even if you don't speak a particular language, you can often use the same techniques in English that are traditional to the other language. So when composing an invocation to the Celtic god Lugh, you might write a poem rich in internal rhymes; an invocation to the Chinese goddess Kuan Yin could take the form of prose sprinkled with quotes from Buddhist scripture.

For each composition you write, you need to select just the right combination of tools. Too few, and the words won't hang together; too many, and they get in each other's way. Some forms of writing tell you what techniques to use in them. Others leave you more free choice. Study your options and see which you like best.

Sound Effects

Writers use sounds to delight the ear. Some sounds are fun to hear and say. Groups of sounds can stir different emotions. Repeated sounds work similar to the punch line of a joke—your brain starts to expect certain things, so that echoes and surprises yield a sense of satisfaction. Here are some sound effects that can jazz up your writing.

Onomatopoeia

Onomatopoeia is basically a fancy name for words that sound like what they mean: buzz, hiccup, snap. Magical examples abound, such as "popping off a spell" or "zapping it with a magic wand." Some deities are associated with particular animals, and animal sounds may be used to invoke them. For example, *mau* is the Egyptian word for "cat" and *Pasht* (meaning "she who tears") is the name of a goddess with cat and lioness attributes, believed to be a merger of Bast and Sekhmet. Both terms resemble noises made by felines, and both are used in Egyptian magical and spiritual practices.

Alliteration

Alliteration repeats consonant sounds at the beginnings of words, "like listening to lovely lyrics." It carries considerable weight in a composition, drawing the audience's attention, especially when read out loud. The more times you repeat a sound, the more powerful the effect; two or three can be subtle, and four or more creates a driving force.

Old English poetry made frequent use of alliteration—far more than it used rhyme—a feature shared by all the older Germanic languages. The technique fell out of fashion for centuries, but has recently made a comeback. Alliteration and its relatives work particularly well in ritual poetry. In prose, they offer a more discreet unifying factor than rhyme, ideal for situations when you want a tight connection, but you don't want to draw too much attention to it.

Consonance

Consonance repeats consonant sounds in the middle or at the end of words, "in sequential or uncommon cycles." Its effect is subtler than alliteration, although it grows stronger the more repetition you add. Alliteration and consonance work well together. You can combine them to make the effect more pronounced or more discreet, depending on how you choose to arrange the sounds.

Assonance

Assonance repeats vowel sounds at the beginnings of words or inside of words, "only opening potent overtures of hope." At the beginning, it works the way alliteration does; in the middle, it works the way consonance does. Where consonant sounds can create an aggressive tone, vowels seem more gentle and flowing. A composition rich in assonance pours forth in an almost unbroken stream of sound. This technique combines well with consonance and alliteration too.

Rhyme

Rhyme repeats sounds at the ends of words, "especially fine | at the end of a line." *Internal rhymes* fall within a line of poetry. The simplest rhyme is a matching vowel sound, such as "go" and "snow." It creates an open, flowing sense similar to assonance. Closely related is a rhyme with the same vowel and consonant sound, such as "sleep" and "reap." This gives a more assertive conclusion to the line.

The above are examples of *perfect rhyme*, also called true rhyme. The final vowels (and if present, final consonants) of the words must sound exactly the same. However, there is another kind of rhyme, called *imperfect rhyme,* near rhyme, or off rhyme. In this case the sounds are similar but not identical, usually varying either the vowel or the consonant, such as "night" and "flights" or "keep" and "coop." Imperfect rhyme can work very well on its own, when used throughout a poem; it gives a slightly muffled effect that plucks at the audience's subconscious. Using an imperfect rhyme because you can't think of a perfect one, however, is poor form—you can get away with it in ritual poetry, where magical function counts more than literary precision, but try to avoid this.

Rhymes can also be characterized by syllable count and stress. The *masculine rhymes* usually have one syllable (but may have more) and the stress falls on the final syllable, such as "detain" and "refrain." In contrast, *feminine rhymes* have two syllables, with the stress falling on the first syllable, and both syllables must match, such as "patter" and "matter." The trisyllabic rhymes have three syllables, all of which must match, such as "hovering" and "covering." Perhaps the most interesting are *mosaic rhymes,* in which one word rhymes with two or more other words, as in "retribution" and "you shun."

Masculine rhymes give a more emphatic end to a line; the other rhymes suggest carryover. Trisyllabic and mosaic rhymes appear mainly in humorous verse, although they can work in a serious context. Feminine rhymes can go either way, depending how you use them. You can also mix and match these types within a single poem; alternating masculine and feminine lines is a popular choice.

The above sound effects are "echo" techniques; they help tie a poem together through repetition. This generates power and aids memorization. If you use them more than a little bit, they create a strong sense of expectation in the audience. You can also play against this to raise tension—because couplets and quatrains are more common, rhymed tercets tend to surprise people. For similar effect, try switching between alliteration and assonance from one line or verse to another.

Here is a comparison of alliteration, assonance, and consonance along with perfect rhyme for contrast:

Name	Example	First sound	Middle sound	End sound
Rhyme	honey, sunny	different	same	same
Assonance	chime, flight	different	same	different
Consonance	peace, grass renew, anoint	different different	different same	same different
Alliteration	my, mother	same	different	different

Rhythm and Meter

Rhythm concerns the pattern of sounds in a composition. It can be irregular or regular. Irregular rhythm concerns the rise and fall of words, their overall pacing and emphasis in a composition—without imposing a specific structure. Most prose features irregular rhythm: a natural flow to the words, without the driving beat that characterizes some poetry. A regular rhythm follows a consistent *meter,* a specific sequence of stressed and unstressed syllables in the words, rather like a tune in music. Poetic forms often specify a meter, though not all do so. Most ritual poetry benefits from a strong and regular rhythm, which helps raise and direct energy as well as making the words easier to memorize.

The basic unit of measuring meter is called a *foot.* It consists of two or three syllables, usually a combination of stressed and unstressed. Each foot's name indicates its number of syllables and their stress pattern. A stressed, or accented, syllable is marked with this: ´. An unstressed syllable is marked with this: ˘. Here are some feet with their names, accent marks, and examples.[1]

iamb (iambic)	˘ ´	ópĕn
trochee (trochaic)	˘ ´	rĕtúrn
pyrrhus (pyrrhic)	˘ ˘	ĭn ă
spondee (spondaic)	´ ´	blúe-gréen
anapest (anapestic)	˘ ˘ ´	ŏn thĕ flóor
dactyl (dactylic)	´ ˘ ˘	gállŏpĭng
bacchus (bacchic)	˘ ´ ´	ă cóld níght
antibacchus (antibacchic)	´ ´ ˘	wárm bréezĕs
amphibrach	˘ ´ ˘	bĕtwéen thĕ
amphimacer	´ ˘ ´	úndĕr gróund

Some feet have noteworthy characteristics. The iambic foot has become especially popular because the English language tends to fall into this pattern naturally. The anapestic foot gives a swift, cantering beat useful for raising energy. Conversely, the dactylic foot falls away from its initial stress, useful in dispersing energy. The spondaic foot slows the rhythm and creates a sense of gravity.[2]

Line length also plays an important role in rhythm. Special words count the number of feet per line:

monometer	one foot
dimeter	two feet
trimeter	three feet
tetrameter	four feet
pentameter	five feet
hexameter	six feet
heptameter	seven feet
octameter	eight feet
nonameter	nine feet
decameter	ten feet

Thus, we can describe the meter of a sonnet as iambic pentameter: a poem whose lines each have five feet consisting of one unstressed syllable followed by one stressed syllable. Very short lines are harder to write; very long ones are harder to read and remember. Tetrameter, pentameter, and hexameter tend to balance.

If this sounds complicated, don't panic. It's more important to understand the concepts than to memorize their names. The formal names for poetic feet and their numbers have two main uses: (1) analyzing and discussing poetry, and (2) defining a form so that poets can write in it. In such contexts, the names are precise and convenient; otherwise, you probably won't need them much.

Break points also affect rhythm. An *end-stopped* line concludes with a pause, often marked with a comma or period. A run-on line does not end with a pause, but continues straight into the next line; this is called *enjambment*. Within a line, a pause is called a *caesura*, sometimes noted with a pair of vertical lines: ||. Ritual poetry may use any of these, but end-stopped lines come down with a terrific thump, like driving a tent stake into the ground; this helps direct your magic where you want it.

However, poetry in the ear can accommodate a more flexible rhythm than poetry on the written page, so you can discreetly add or drop a syllable here and there, provided that it does not sound forced. Listen to folk ballads or modern pop songs and you'll hear a lot of this. It works far better with unstressed syllables than with stressed syllables, though. People are more likely to stumble over an extra or missing stress.

By the way, it is perfectly acceptable to use study aids for these concepts. Count out the syllables of a poem on your fingers if that helps you keep track. Read it out loud over and over again. Print it out and fill in the accent marks so that you can see the stresses. Write the number of feet or syllables per line. Anything that makes it easier for you to understand ritual or poetic theory, analyze someone else's material, or compose your own, is legitimate.

In ritual prose, sound effects need to be subtler than in poetry. Prose doesn't have specific line breaks, or rhymes. But you can control the pacing with word choice, sentence structure, and pauses. Short words and simple sentences speed up the pace; longer words and complex sentences slow it down. A pause can emphasize what is to follow it, or allow time to absorb what preceded it.

Literal Language

Language can be literal or figurative. Literal language describes things as they actually are. This helps ground you and your audience in reality. Literal language includes concrete and abstract concepts, sense imagery, and parallels.

Concrete vs. Abstract

Concrete and *abstract* concepts exist on a spectrum. Toward one end lie specific things we can touch, such as "water." Toward the other end lie broad categories, such as "animal" and ephemeral concepts, such as "hope." Both have their uses in magical writing.

Most of the time, concrete words strengthen a composition. For example, use "oak" instead of "tree" or "plant," and use "Artemis" instead of "Goddess of Love" or "higher power." This helps you connect to the particular subject of your composition. In group work, it tightens the focus so that everyone's visualization is similar. Vague descriptions allow the imagery, and thus the energy, to scatter.

Sometimes, however, abstract words can prove useful. For example, abstraction is much more inclusive, an advantage during interfaith ceremonies, or rituals to aid a large and diverse group of people. Also, archetypes are a kind of abstraction: The Sky Father is a mystical combination of all masculine parents and celestial phenomena. Many deities oversee an abstract concept such as love, honor, or prosperity.

Sense Imagery

Sense imagery uses perceptual cues to pull listeners into a composition. Nouns ("silk"), verbs ("sing"), adjectives ("radiant"), and adverbs ("quickly") can all evoke a specific sense. Imagery uses the audience's own memories, both positive and negative, to generate emotions in relation to the composition.

For hearing, encourage your audience to listen by describing things to hear, such as wind blowing through leaves. All of the sound-based techniques, just as rhyme and rhythm, affect this area as well. Onomatopoeia and sound effects, such as humming or howling, makes a nice alternative to matching sounds.

For sights, smells, and flavors, use vivid adjectives. Make them as precise as possible: not "blue," but "turquoise"; not "floral," but "rosy"; not "sweet," but "honeyed." Paint a picture with words. Offer the reader something to see, sniff, taste. Also pay attention to the appearance of the composition on the page, how its words and spaces invite the eye. In poetry, use the line breaks to your advantage. In prose, break long sections into smaller, more manageable pieces.

Strong verbs and adverbs convey motion and feeling. Again, aim for precise and powerful terms: not "run," but "gallop"; not "say," but "whisper"; not "join," but "braid." Stir things up! Make your audience tap their feet in time to your words. Tell them what moves and changes and evolves in your composition. In spells and rituals, especially, you may include directions for people to follow: "Raise your hands up to the sky / Look the Goddess in the eye!"

Metaphysical senses pose a greater challenge, because not everyone shares the same perceptions—or even interprets a given input the same way. However, some things remain fairly consistent. Auras are usually perceived through magical sight, appearing as a glow or color(s). Divine messages may be heard; danger alerts often manifest as alarm bells or sirens. Magic itself can often be felt as a tingle or heat. Empathy entails sensing another person's emotional state.

Physical and metaphysical images have different advantages and disadvantages. The physical senses offer the most familiarity, as almost everyone shares the same set. Metaphysical senses come in a wider diversity, but vary radically from one person to another. Some people find the similarity of the former confirming; others find it boring. Some prefer the freedom of metaphysical description; others consider it confusing. Explore both aspects of imagery.

Cast these perceptions in elegant terms and you have a basis for good magical writing. For a love spell you might say, "The warmth of your regard fills me like sunlit honey." Because metaphysical senses lack much vocabulary of their own, their description overlaps the figurative as well as the literal—they are often described in simile and metaphor.

Parallels (Anaphora)

Parallels repeat a phrase or line at intervals throughout a composition. In poetry, *anaphora* (from Greek, meaning "a carrying up or back") refers to a kind of parallel in which multiple lines each begin with the same word or phrase. This appears especially often in blessings. You can see parallels in Bible verses, and many other examples of devotional poetry and prose. The Declaration of Independence—which created the thoughtform "The United States of America"—features a splendid list of parallels detailing the offenses of King George, each beginning with "He has...." This is one of the world's oldest literary techniques.

Figurative Language

Figurative language says things in a more oblique or colorful way than everyday speech. Some of its writing tricks fall into a fairly esoteric realm, but others are common. Most appear in prose as well as poetry, though they may appear more frequently in the latter. You can add to the mystery and excitement of magical composition by using appropriate figures of speech, such as allusion, kennings, metonymy and synecdoche, personification, simile and metaphor, symbolism, and synaesthesia.

Allusion

Allusion refers to another work assumed familiar to the audience, such as "Come on, Romeo, let's finish this project and then you can go find your girlfriend!" or, "She reminded me of Stonehenge, ancient and a bit worn, but still powerful." It offers a type of shorthand, allowing you to describe a subject by calling up a host of associations based on some other thing. Myths and legends offer a rich source of possible allusions.

Epithets

Names hold a special magic of their own. *Epithets* are descriptive titles or phrases that often appear in association with powerful entities. Examples from mythology and literature include "fleet-footed Artemis," "the Horned One," "Gandalf the Grey," and so forth. Use traditional or original epithets in invocations, prayers, blessings, and other compositions involving higher powers.

Kennings

Kennings are picturesque phrases with a mystical flair, used in Anglo-Saxon and other European legends and poems to represent especially important things—heroes, queens, wizards, artifacts, weapons, natural features, and so on. Many of these have been passed down for centuries and evoke a sense of rolling grandeur. For inspiration, take "swan-road" for migratory route, "world-candle" for sun, "giver of golden rings" for king.

Metonymy and Synecdoche

Metonymy and *synecdoche* both involve substituting one word for another. Metonymy replaces the subject with an associated object; for example, "the Round Table" refers to the knights of King Arthur who sat around that famous piece of furniture. Synecdoche uses different aspects of the subject, such as one part referring to the whole ("all *hands* on deck" for summoning sailors), a broad category referring to a narrow example ("milk" for cow's milk), or the material of the subject referring to the subject itself ("copper" for penny). Such references add grandeur and mystery, avoid repetition, and make it possible to avoid naming entities whose proper names are not to be used casually. Thus, in a magical tradition in which certain members belt their robes with a green cord, someone might write, "Green cords form a circle," to indicate who creates the circle.

Personification

Personification attributes human qualities to anything non-human such as an animal ("Cats laugh at us when we call them"), object ("The Moon watches us as we come, her bright face smiling down"), or idea ("Love is blind"). Such qualities include emotions, body language, physical senses, deliberate actions, and speech. From a magical perspective, everything has some kind of awareness or spirit, and so this technique appears frequently in magical compositions.

Simile and Metaphor

Similes and *metaphors* compare different things based on some degree of similarity. Similes compare objects or ideas to each other using the words "like" or "as"; for example, "The Sun God's kiss burned like fire." Metaphors directly equate different concepts, for instance, "The wizard stood steadfast, a mountain against onrushing wind." Invent original comparisons if you wish, but in this context, it's perfectly fine to use ancient ones such as "white as snow" when they suit your purpose.

Symbolism

Symbolism uses familiar objects or designs to represent abstract qualities; for example, a lightning bolt suggests speed and power. Such substitutions prove especially effective in magical compositions because the listeners are usually familiar with the idea of correspondences. Colors, directions, seasons, artifacts, animals, plants, and many other things work well for this.

Synaesthesia

Synaesthesia involves a crossover between two or more senses. For example, you might have "a rosy outlook on life," although your outlook is neither pink nor floral-scented. Synaesthesia can be purely figurative, a way of describing ordinary things in a new and interesting way. However, it can also be literal; some individuals perceive sounds as colors, and magical senses often overlap physical senses. Spells with mind-altering effects (such as love spells) and prayers to deities of intoxication (such as Bacchus) often employ synaesthesia.

On Balance and Analysis

Opinions differ as to the best way to analyze compositions. The divide falls between the objective analysis of someone else's writing, and the subjective analysis of one's own writing. The advantage of objective analysis is dispassion; it allows the reader to consider the work for its own sake, and investigate what the writer might have meant by it, without insider knowledge. The disadvantage is that it's hard to check the results, because one can never know what the writer *really* meant—unless he or she left notes to that effect, or the analysis takes place in a writer's group. Sometimes readers get quite different impressions from a composition than the writer intended! The advantage of subjective analysis is that the authors know exactly what they meant to say, what they did, and how they did it. The disadvantage is that they don't know how well it works for readers unconnected to the work and its context in the author's mind—unless they solicit feedback from an audience (and they're lucky enough to get some that is both honest and detailed enough to be useful).

In order to develop talent and skill fully, every writer needs to master both types of analysis. Exploring the works of other authors allows the student to learn new skills and to appreciate those who have gone before. Examining one's own work allows writers to observe their growing skill in composition, figure out what makes a composition work (or not work), and improve their writing. Teachers, scholars, and writers generally agree that both types of analysis are important.

The catch is that people differ over which type should be used in educational and publication contexts. The academic community has a pretty firm bias against analyzing one's own work to demonstrate a point. Conversely, the creative community often balks at "shredding" or even "interpreting" the work of another writer in public, preferring to use examples from the author's own material. Both sides have valid points.

In the interest of balance, this book features sample compositions drawn from my personal work, from older works in the public domain, and a few more contributed by contemporary writers. Further examples of materials currently under copyright, especially songs on albums, are referenced but not reproduced in the text, and may be looked up in their respective sources. Readers are encouraged to explore the examples in this book, and to apply their analytical skills to their own writing.

Exercises

Use the following exercises to practice with the tools and techniques presented in this chapter. You do not need to do all of them; it's okay to pick and choose. You may want to revisit these after you've read later chapters on specific types of writing, and combine them with other exercises.

Exercise #1: Testing Your Tools

Find out whether and how your tools affect your work. Remember that the power is really in you, not in your tools; but the right tools may make certain things easier. First, choose two different versions of a tool, such as an ordinary pen and a fancy Pen of Art. Then write a short composition with each of them, such as your thoughts on empowering magical tools. Did you find it easier to work with a certain tool? Did one of them channel power better? You may want to repeat this exercise, replacing one of the tools with a computer.

Exercise #2: Hitting the Books

Make a list of your favorite magical words—athame, banish, circle, deosil, familiar, invoke, mojo, occult, pentacle, rune, scry, visualize, wand, and so on. Gather several of your reference books: a dictionary, encyclopedia, rhyming dictionary, and thesaurus. (These can be ordinary books, books with a magical focus, or a combination of the two.) Start with the first word, and look it up in each book. Compare the information you found. Then look up the other words. What did you learn? How could you use this information in magical composition?

Exercise #3: Techniques in Poetry

Read the following poem and the discussion of the techniques it features. Several additional poems appear after the set of exercises; choose three of them and identify as many of their techniques as you can.

"Sleep" by Sir Philip Sidney

Come, Sleep; O Sleep! the certain knot of peace,
The baiting-place of wit, the balm of woe,
The poor man's wealth, the prisoner's release,
Th' indifferent judge between the high and low;
With shield of proof shield me from out the prease
Of those fierce darts Despair at me doth throw:
O make in me those civil wars to cease;
I will good tribute pay, if thou do so.
Take thou of me smooth pillows, sweetest bed,
A chamber deaf to noise and blind of light,
A rosy garland and a weary head;
And if these things, as being thine by right,
Move not thy heavy grace, thou shalt in me,
Livelier than elsewhere, Stella's image see.

Discussion: This poem begins with the personification of "Sleep" as something that can hear entreaties. It would make a good spell for relieving insomnia. "Sleep," "Sleep," and "peace" are examples of assonance; so are "baiting" and "place." "The certain knot of peace," "the baiting-place of wit," "the balm of woe," "the poor man's wealth," "the prisoner's release," and "th' indifferent judge between high and low" are all kennings for sleep. "Shield of proof," "those fierce darts Despair at me doth throw," and "civil wars" are all metaphors. "Despair" is another personification. "Smooth pillows," "sweetest bed," "a chamber deaf to noise and blind of light," "a rosy garland," and "a weary head" are all sense images. "Sweetest bed" is also synaesthesia; a bed would normally be described by texture, but is here given a flavor. "Heavy grace" and "Stella's image" return to sense imagery. The meter is iambic pentameter.

Exercise #4: Techniques in Prose

Read the following myth and the discussion of what techniques it features. Another myth appears after the set of exercises; identify as many of its techniques as you can.

"The Battle of the Wizards"
by Frances Jenkins Olcott

BOOM! BOOM! BOOM! BEAT! BEAT! BEAT! Listen to Nischergurgje!

Far, far away in Lapland of the Many Wizards, beyond the Arctic Circle, in mid-winter, it is one Long Night. But what a night!

There is silence. The stars sparkle in the vast, dark sky. A soft white shimmer glows over the fields of ice and snow covering tundra, valley, and hill. Deep ice binds the lakes and streams.

Then see! Upward across the sky sweep wondrous lights. Amber-colored veils shimmer to and fro, rosy draperies, garlands, and streamers red, orange, yellow, green, blue, and violet, dart, dance, sway, shift, wave, and leap across the sky; flare up and die down, then spring up again woven all of rainbow colors.

And the little, dark children of Lapland of the many Wizards and much Magic, are filled with mystery. They listen for the Call of the Magic Drum, and they watch the Aurora Lights, and say:

"See! the warriors are fighting!"

In the long, long ago, the Wizard Nischergurgje,

chanting Magic Spells with whistlings and drum-beatings, came wandering over the frozen marshes. Under a crooked pine tree he sat down to rest, and to boil his dinner of reindeer flesh.

And while he was waiting for the cooking pot to simmer, he heard something creak—crack—creak above his head. He looked up. Through the crooked boughs, an evil face grinned at him. It was Schlipme's—the Wicked Wizard of the Wicked Moon Daughter.

Then Nischergurgje quickly muttered a Spell, and the Wicked Wizard tumbled to the ground.

"Wicked Schlipme," said the Great Wizard, "Servant of the Wicked Moon Daughter, of the caved-in forehead, crooked mouth, and pale, cruel lips that splutter curses! See! My Spell has taken from you all your power."

"Nischergurgje," snarled the Wicked Wizard, "my Magic is still strong. I can call on the Moon Spirits to destroy you."

"Your Black Art does not frighten me," answered Nischergurgje.

Then the Wicked Schlipme stood up, and by his Black Art grew and grew, taller and taller, to great stature. In his hand he swung a terrible club made of a spruce tree.

"I will grind you to powder as fine as the snow on the hillside," he roared. "Tremble before me!"

"See what my Good Magic will do!" said Nischergurgje.

And he muttered a Spell, and he, too, grew and grew, taller and taller and yet taller. Greater he was than the Wicked Wizard. The tallest pines in the forest scarce reached his knees. The highest peaks of the mountains scarce touched his waist. His chest and shoulders were hid among the clouds. His chin pushed the moon. His eyes glared into the sun.

"You have taken my strength from me!" cried Schlipme in fear.

Then they changed themselves into dreadful Storm Clouds. They rushed upon each other. They closed in fierce combat. A mighty roaring was heard. The sky was black.

Nischergurgje uttered a terrible Spell, and Schlipme fell in a heap to earth.

"Again you have taken my strength from me!" cried the Wicked Wizard.

Once more the two Wizards changed their forms. They became two great, horned reindeer. They battled over the frozen snow of the hillside. The whole forest echoed with the loud clashing of their antlers. The trampling of their hoofs shook the earth.

Then the Wicked Wizard was too weak to fight more. He changed himself into a great snake writhing on the ground. Nischergurgje, too, became a snake. They twined and twisted. Their angry hissing could be heard afar off. Their dripping fangs were dreadful to see.

Then suddenly the Wicked Wizard stretched himself upon the ground as if dead. In the twinkling of an eye he became a mighty bird. He soared in wide circles about the Great Wizard, who was still a snake.

But Nischergurgje took the form of an eagle. He rose swiftly in the air. He overtook the Wicked Schlipme, and sank his claws into his back. He brought him down to earth.

Then Wicked Schlipme, bleeding and torn, howled: "Now you have taken all my strength!"

And he sank down, down, into the dark Under Earth Land.

Nischergurgje went back to beat his Magic Drum

and to cook his supper of reindeer flesh.
While over his head, across the deep dark sky,
flashed and shimmered the many colored Northern
Lights red, orange, yellow, green, blue, and violet.
And the little brown Children of Lapland cried out:
"See! The warriors are fighting!"

Discussion: "BOOM!" and "BEAT!" are onomatopoeia, and the repeating "b" is alliteration. Assonance subtly ties together the story, as with the short "i" of "in," "Many," "Wizards," "Arctic," "mid-winter," "it," and "is." Sense imagery includes "silence," "stars sparkle," "vast, dark sky," "soft white shimmer glows," and "ice binds," plus the litany of colors at the end: "red, orange, yellow, green, blue, and violet." "Children of Lapland," "Wicked Wizard," and "Great Wizard" are all epithets. "Amber-colored veils" and "rosy draperies" are metaphors. "Wicked Moon Daughter" is personification, and the whole story personifies the Aurora Borealis as two warriors fighting. "As fine as the snow" is simile.

Exercise #5: Practicing Techniques

Choose three techniques from this chapter and explore each in depth. For each of these, write at least one composition (in any form) that uses that technique. In one composition, replicate the general flavor of some ethnic tradition. In another composition, capture the mood of a specific season. In the third composition, write about a deity or other higher power. (You may do this exercise now, or double back to it after reading about forms in later chapters.)

Exercise #6: Compare and Contrast

Some techniques are closely related to each other—alliteration, assonance, and consonance; rhythm and meter; concrete and abstract; metonymy and synecdoche; simile and metaphor. Choose one such set and write about the similarities and differences between those techniques.

Exercise #7: Practicing Comparisons

Choose a different set of related techniques than you used in Exercises #5 and #6. Write three compositions (in any form). Use one technique in the first composition, a related technique in the second composition, and both techniques in the third composition. How well do those techniques work together, and separately? (You may do this exercise now, or double back to it after reading about forms in later chapters.)

Sample Poems Illustrating Techniques

"Aishah Shechinah"
by Robert Stephen Hawker
A shape, like folded light, embodied air,
Yet wreathed with flesh, and warm:
All that of heaven is feminine and fair,
Moulded in visible form,

She stood, the Lady Shechinah of earth,
A chancel for the sky:
Where woke, to breath and beauty, God's own Birth,
For men to see Him by.

Round her, too pure to mingle with the day,
Light, that was life, abode;
Folded within her fibres meekly lay
The link of boundless God.

So linked, so blent, that when, with pulse fulfilled,
Moved but that Infant Hand,
Far, far away, His conscious Godhead thrilled,
And stars might understand.

Lo! where they pause, with inter-gathering rest,
The Threefold, and the One;
And lo, He binds them to her orient breast,
His manhood girded on.

The zone, where two glad worlds for ever meet,
Beneath that bosom ran:
Deep in that womb the conquering Paraclete
Smote Godhead on to man.

Sole scene among the stars, where, yearning, glide
The Threefold and the One;
Her God upon her lap, the Virgin Bride,
Her awful Child, her Son!

"Amergin" by Anonymous

I am the wind which breathes upon the sea,
I am the wave of the ocean,
I am the murmur of the billows,
I am the ox of the seven combats,
I am the vulture upon the rocks,
I am a beam of the sun,
I am the fairest of plants,
I am a wild boar in valour,
I am a salmon in the water,
I am a lake in the plain,
I am a word of science,
I am the point of the lance in battle,
I am the God who creates in the head the fire.
Who is it who throws light into the meeting on the mountain?
Who announces the ages of the moon?
Who teaches the place where couches the sun?

"Excalibur" by Sallie Bridges

For months it rested in the stone,
    The sword Excalibur;
The noblest knights of England's realm
    Strove hard the steel to stir;
For word had gone through all the land
    That he who drew the blade

Should fill the sovereign's empty throne,
> The rightful king be made.

The flower of island chivalry
> Had come from far and near,
To try their skill at tournament
> The first day of the year.
Mid the barons went Sir Ector,
> His valiant son, Sir Kaye,
And his foster-child, young Arthur,
> Forth to the courtly fray.

Unknown to all, dead Uther's son
> Mix'd with the noble throng,
Who dream'd not that to stripling page
> Could crown and throne belong.
"Now, grammercy," quoth Arthur,
> In riding by Sir Kaye,
"Good brother mine, how came you out
> Without a sword to-day?"

Sir Kaye look'd down, and paled to see
> No weapon at his side:
Then back his comrade spurr'd his steed,
> Across the meadows wide,
To where lay idle in its sheath
> The knight's forgotten blade,
But found that not a single squire
> Had in the castle stay'd.

Quoth Arthur then, with sudden wrath,
> "From yonder mystic stone
I'll pluck the sword, that good Sir Kaye
> May wield it as his own!"
So, lighting down from off his horse,
> Towards the empty tent
In which was kept Excalibur
> His eager footsteps bent.

In golden-letter'd hilt was bright,
    Its knightly guards away;
And so, with brave and fearless heart,
    He made his bold essay.
He grasp'd the handle in his hand,
    Its point leap'd sharp and free.
"My brother shall not go unarm'd
    To battle now!" cried he.

When old Sir Ector saw the blade
    Flash in the morning light,
He knew it was the Sword of Fate
    That met his wondering sight,
And ask'd of Arthur, "Whither came
    The steel thou gavest Sir Kaye?"
"I bore it," was the plain reply,
    "From stone and tent away."

"Then, by my faith," the gray knight swore,
    "An' thou canst draw again
The sword from out the selfsame place,
    A monarch thou shalt reign!"
And back within the marble stone
    Prince Arthur thrust the blade,
While long in vain to pluck it thence
    Both high and low essay'd.

"Come hither; strive again, my son!"
    And quick on Ector's sight,
In Arthur's hand, the marvellous steel
    Was flashing keen and bright.
Then kneel'd Sir Ector and Sir Kaye,
    With every squire and lord,
To greet as lawful king the youth
    Who lean'd upon the Sword!

Then spoke his aged foster-sire.
    "Ye hail no child of mine!"

But wist not buried Uther's heir
    Was king by right divine.
Thus Arthur through Excalibur
    Received his father's crown;
And ever through Excalibur
    He kept his high renown!

"Hymn to Diana" by Ben Jonson

QUEEN and huntress, chaste and fair,
Now the sun is laid to sleep,
Seated in thy silver chair,
State in wonted manner keep:
Hesperus entreats thy light,
Goddess excellently bright.

Earth, let not thy envious shade
Dare itself to interpose;
Cynthia's shining orb was made
Heaven to clear when day did close:
Bless us then with wishèd sight,
Goddess excellently bright.

Lay thy bow of pearl apart,
And thy crystal-shining quiver;
Give unto the flying hart
Space to breathe, how short soever:
Thou that mak'st a day of night-
Goddess excellently bright.

"Immortality" by A.E.

We must pass like smoke or live within the spirit's fire;
For we can no more than smoke unto the flame return
If our thought has changed to dream, our will unto desire,
As smoke we vanish though the fire may burn.

Lights of infinite pity star the grey dusk of our days:
Surely here is soul: with it we have eternal breath:
In the fire of love we live, or pass by many ways,
By unnumbered ways of dream to death.

"The Shadow House of Lugh" by Ethna Carbery

Dream-fair, besides dream waters, it stands alone:
A winged thought of Lugh made its corner stone:
A desire of his heart raised its walls on high,
And set its crystal windows to flaunt the sky.

Its doors of the white bronze are many and bright,
With wonderous carven pillars for his Love's delight,
And its roof of the blue wings, the speckled red,
Is a flaming arc of beauty above her head.

Like a mountain through mist Lugh towers high,
The fiery-forked lightning is the glance of his eye,
His countenance is noble as the Sun-god's face—
The proudest chieftain he of a proud De Danaan race.

He bides there in peace now, his wars are all done—
He gave his hand to Balor when the death gate was won,
And for the strife-scarred heroes who wander in the
shade,
His door lieth open, and the rich feast is laid.

He hath no vexing memory of blood in slanting rain,
Of green spears in hedges on a battle plain;
But through the haunted quiet his Love's silver words
Blow round him swift as wing-beats of enchanted birds.

A grey haunted wind is blowing in the hall,
And stirring through the shadowy spears upon the wall,
The drinking-horn goes round from shadowy lip to lip—
And about the golden methers shadowy fingers slip.

The Star of Beauty, she who queens it there;
Diademed, and wondrous long, her yellow hair.
Her eyes are twin-moons in a rose-sweet face,
And the fragrance of her presence fills all the place.

He plays for her pleasure on his harp's gold wire
The laughter-tune that leaps along in trills of fire;

> She hears the dancing feet of Sidhe where a white
> moon gleams,
> And all her world is joy in the House of Dreams.
>
> He plays for her soothing the Slumber-song:
> Fine and faint as any dream it glides along:
> She sleeps until the magic of his kiss shall rouse;
> And all her world is quiet in the Shadow-house.
>
> His days glide to night, and his nights glide to day:
> With circling of the amber mead, and feasting gay;
> In the yellow of her hair his dreams lie curled,
> And her arms make the rim of his rainbow world.

Lugh is the Celtic divinity whose name is most widely known. In mythology he is the Sun God. In the mythological cycle he is the deliverer of the De Danaans from the Fomorian oppression. He is the slayer of Balor, the glance of whose eye is death. But Lugh is also kin to Balor, his mother being Eithlinn, the daughter whom Balor had immured like Danae in a tower.

"A Song of Freedom" by Alice Mulligan

> In Cavan of little lakes,
> As I was walking with the wind,
> And no one seen beside me there,
> There came a song into my mind;
> It came as if the whispered voice
> Of one, but none of human kind,
> Who walked with me in Cavan then,
> And he invisible as wind.
>
> On Urris of Inish-Owen,
> As I went up the mountain side,
> The brook that came leaping down
> Cried to me—for joy it cried;
> And when from off the summit far
> I looked o'er land and water wide,
> I was more joyous than the brook

That met me on the mountain side.
To Ara of Connacht's isles,
As I went sailing o'er the sea,
The wind's word, the brook's word,
The wave's word, was plain to me—
As we are, though she is not,
As we are, shall Banba be—
There is no king can rule the wind,
There is no fetter for the sea.

"Spring" by Thomas Nashe
Spring, the sweet Spring, is the year's pleasant king;
Then blooms each thing, then maids dance in a ring,
Cold doth not sting, the pretty birds do sing—
Cuckoo, jug-jug, pu-we, to-witta-woo!

The palm and may make country houses gay,
Lambs frisk and play, the shepherds pipe all day,
And we hear aye birds tune this merry lay—
Cuckoo, jug-jug, pu-we, to-witta-woo!

The fields breathe sweet, the daisies kiss our feet,
Young lovers meet, old wives a-sunning sit,
In every street these tunes our ears do greet—
Cuckoo, jug-jug, pu-we, to-witta-woo!
Spring, the sweet Spring!

Chapter Four: Making Magical Poetry— Basic Forms

In order to write poetry, including magical poetry, you need to become familiar with forms. A poetic *form* consists of a specific set of rules for writing a poem. The form usually stipulates a poem's rhyme pattern (or lack thereof), and often the meter. It may also control the number of lines, syllables per line, and stanzas. These influence the shape of the poem on the page, which can also be part of the form unto itself. Certain techniques may be required, such as alliteration or parallels, as described in Chapter Three.

The basic unit of form is the *stanza,* or verse: a group of lines that go together, with individual stanzas separated by blank lines. Each stanza may contain a separate idea, or they may flow together to create a unified narrative. Within a stanza, the *line* is a smaller unit, consisting of a row of words with a deliberate beginning and end, unlike prose where line breaks are not tightly controlled. Lines can emphasize rhymes, compare or contrast ideas, and set up a change in tone. Within a line, the foot determines meter, as discussed in the last chapter. This establishes the poem's rhythm.

Thus, the form is the underlying structure of a poem. It gives shape to the message, much as your skeleton gives shape to your body. Unlike prose, poetry is written in verse, and a poem may have one stanza or many. The author creates each line as a distinct segment of the whole, instead of letting line breaks fall where they may, and arranges the lines in a specific way. The pattern of words, poetic techniques, and lines all follow the chosen form.

When planning poetry, pick a form that works well for the purpose and type of your composition. Do you want something long or short? Formal or casual? With or without rhyme and meter? Does an ethnic connection or other aspect suggest a specific form? Note any form requirements such as rhyme pattern or number of syllables per line.

When in doubt, try one to three verses of the ballad form described here. That suits almost any purpose. If you get bored with ballads, switch to a more exotic form as described in Chapter Five. Explore! Experiment! Don't be afraid to make mistakes. If you don't like the results, you can always backtrack and try something else later.

When composing poetry, take advantage of the snowball effect. Often you can build a whole poem around one or two really catchy lines. If you get stuck for synonyms, pull out your thesaurus. For rhyme trouble, use a rhyming dictionary to expand your options. Pick words and phrases from your notes and look them up to see if anything else on the list of rhymes for that sound might relate to your topic. Then design lines around those.

When writing a poem that rhymes, pay careful attention to sentence structure. English can withstand a certain amount of juggling the word order to put a rhyme where you need it, but there are limits. "'Come,' I said, 'with me!'" works as well as "'Come with me!' I said," but "I said, 'With me come!'" sounds silly. If you need to match a rhyme, consider synonyms for different words, see whether adding or deleting whole phrases might help, and use your rhyming dictionary.

When revising poetry, bear in mind that a poem may deviate from ordinary rules. If you're writing a poem that doesn't use normal punctuation, you still need to proofread—for consistency within the exceptional rules used for that composition. For example, e.e. cummings customarily wrote poetry (and his name) all in lowercase for a soft, dreamy, whispery effect. Outside such exceptions, revise as normal; only bend the rules when necessary.

Starting Simple

The basic forms share certain features. All of them are both simple and flexible. They have no fixed length or number of stanzas per poem, so they can run long or short as needed. They have a specific rhyme pattern (or exclusion of rhyme, in free verse), but no fixed meter. They may use a wide range of other literary techniques. This makes them relatively easy to write— just enough rules to give your composition some cohesion, but not so many that they get in your way.

The forms presented in this lesson are free verse, couplet, and ballad. Chances are, you already know these. They rank among the most common examples of poetry in English, appearing in many songs and poetic speeches. (Other languages have their own favorite forms, such as haiku in Japanese, which we'll discuss later.) Thus, they appear in reading and writing classes at all levels of education. With these, you can meet pretty much any need for ritual poetry.

Certain conventions enable people to transcribe the rules of a form clearly and precisely, so that poets can create new poems in that form. The meter is described in terms of feet and number, such as "trochaic tetrameter." Rhymes are indicated with lowercase letters, in which repeating letters mean repeating sounds; so that *abcb* means the first and third lines do not rhyme, but the third and fourth lines do rhyme. Repeated words are indicated with capital letters, so that *abcD efgD* would feature the same end word in both stanzas. A single repeated line or phrase may be marked "R," and a set of repeated lines may be marked with several numbered capital letters; you won't need to worry about that until the next chapter, but it's important to include with the other form notations.

Each form appears in its own section below. This includes the name, a description of the form's structure, its historical background, suggestions on how to write it, and a sample poem. If you want to get right to the writing, you may skim over some of the discussion, but reading the whole section will give you a better idea of which forms correspond to which cultures, and which purposes call for which forms.

Free Verse

The *free verse* is the simplest of all poetic forms, in the sense that it has just one rule: Set the line breaks deliberately. The main thing that distinguishes free verse from poetic-sounding prose is this use of specific lines to create one or more stanzas. Lines may be short or long, or may vary in length. Ideas may conclude at the end of each line, or run on to the next line. This form also has no regular pattern of rhyme or meter. It draws instead on the cadence of natural speech, its rhythm flowing and changing throughout. Thus, the basic unit of rhythm is the line, rather than the foot of metrical poetry. However, authors can choose to apply many different literary techniques such as alliteration, sense imagery, parallels, or metaphor. Free verse poetry allows much richer use of figurative language than does prose, in which fancy techniques can become distracting.

You may also encounter this form in its French version, *vers libre*.[1] (Do not confuse free verse with *blank verse*, which is unrhymed iambic pentameter.) Jules Laforgue, Arthur Rimbaud, and others sought to escape the rigidity of French forms and established vers libre as an alternative. In English, free verse dates back to early Anglo-Saxon poetry, a good source for Pagan inspiration. Famous experts of free verse include Maya Angelou, Margaret Atwood, e.e. cummings, Ezra Pound, Adrienne Rich, Henry David Thoreau, and Walt Whitman. More modern terms for free verse include "open form" and "mixed form."

The fluidity of free verse adapts well to any topic and tone. Most poetic forms adapt the content to fit into the form, but free verse adapts the form to the content. Changes in rhythm and line length emphasize important words and ideas. Furthermore, free verse carries the least emotional or cultural baggage of any poetic form. Meandering through many traditions, it belongs to none in particular.

What this means is that you are "free" to make the important decisions about which rules apply to this composition. You might decide to break your poem into stanzas with the same number of lines in each, or an increasing or decreasing number of lines. You might decide to break stanzas with each new thought, using them as you would paragraphs; or where a reader would take a breath, using them as you would commas. You could vary the rhythm from slow and serious to quick and frisky if describing something mutable, such as the weather. You could "hide" rhymes in the middle of lines. It's all up to you.

One way to compose a free verse poem is to start by writing out all of your initial ideas in a single block, similar to a paragraph. Second, break the block into individual lines. Look for places where a break can fit with an existing pause, such as a comma or a period, or where a break can emphasize the last word in a line by splitting a phrase. Experiment with line breaks in different places until you have an arrangement that you like. (Working on a computer makes this easier to do than working on paper, but both methods work.) You can either divide your lines into stanzas, or leave them together in a single stanza. Use stanza breaks to transition from one idea to another, or to break an idea in the middle for emphasis. Next, examine each word to see if it can be replaced with a better one, for stronger imagery, sound effect, or other impact. Delete unnecessary words. Shorter or longer words affect line length, so after this part, check the line breaks again to see if they need adjusting.

Of course, you can also write free verse by inserting line and stanza breaks as you go along. You'll still need to examine your word choices closely, and you may need to change the breaks as your poem evolves.

In a magical context, free verse works well for openings and closings, blessings, or invocations. A sneaky little advantage to free verse is that, if you memorize it but then forget part of it in the midst of a recital, you may manage to ad lib your way to where you remember the rest of it, without anyone noticing. If you flub a rhymed poem, people *will* notice.

The rhyme scheme of free verse looks like this:

abcde...

Here is a sample free verse poem:

"Fog" by Carl Sandburg

The fog comes
on little cat feet.

It sits looking
over harbor and city
on silent haunches
and then moves on.

This simple poem relies on two main techniques, metaphor and personification. The whole thing presents fog as a cat, which is metaphor; but also personification, because a cat is a living thing, so the fog "sits looking" when ordinarily it could not do so. Also, Sandburg cleverly draws on all the abstract associations of "cat" even though only one ("silent") is explicitly mentioned—cats are aloof, mysterious, prone to wandering, capable of getting into surprising places, and so on. This works similarly to a table of correspondences, in which each entry has multiple things linked with it. Once you start thinking "fog = cat," those other associations come along for the ride. So although this poem is quite brief, it contains a lot more concepts hidden "between the lines." There is alliteration in here too: "fog" and "feet," "comes" and "cat," "little" and "looking," "harbor" and "haunches," "city" and "silent."

This poem might prove useful in a spell to clear fog away, or a ceremony honoring a cat goddess such as Bast, or even a ritual having something to do with Chicago. It also demonstrates how much meaning can be crammed into a few lines. Consider how you could use the same techniques to condense ideas for occasions when you don't have the time to read out a long composition.

Couplet

The *couplet* is the shortest verse form, consisting of two-line stanzas whose end words usually rhyme. The poem can have any number of stanzas in it. (Sometimes couplets join together to create four-line stanzas, or even a long poem with no stanza breaks.) Usually the two lines have similar length; different stanzas within the same poem may vary a bit more. The rhythm remains the same throughout the poem.

Many different types of couplets exist, along with some more elaborate forms based on couplet verses. A *closed couplet* completes its idea and syntax by the end. An *open couplet* carries over its idea and syntax to the next couplet. In a *split couplet,* the first line is iambic pentameter, and the second is iambic dimeter. (See Chapter Three for an explanation of meter.) *Short couplets* may be either iambic or trochaic tetrameter. A *couplet envelope* is a six-line stanza in which the first couplet rhymes with the third couplet, a convenient short form. The *elegy* uses dactylic hexameter. The *ghazal* is a form of Arabic, Persian, and Urdu poetry written in couplets. A *heroic couplet* uses iambic pentameter, often with a caesura (pause) in the middle of each line, and an *alexandrine couplet* uses iambic hexameter.

The elegy comes from Greek and Latin.[2] Early poets include Archilochus, Tyrtaeus, and Ennius. Although originally written on a wide range of topics, including military ventures, politics, and philosophy, the elegiac couplet later narrowed its focus to mourning. "Elegy" has come to imply a poem about a deceased person, making this form a natural choice for requiem rituals. However, practitioners of Greek or Roman traditions may wish to explore some of the other historic topics.

The ghazal dates back more than a thousand years, to the 8th century.[3] Originating in Iran, it spread widely. Five to 15 rhyming couplets each contain a complete thought, which can be quite diverse, yet all relating to the same underlying theme. Associated especially with Sufism and other Middle Eastern traditions, the ghazal often uses love or divinity as its central theme. Probably the most famous poet of this form was Rumi, who believed in music, dance, and poetry as pathways to spiritual enlightenment. The rich tradition of this couplet form makes it ideal for magical and spiritual purposes.

Heroic couplets traditionally featured a serious topic and closed stanzas. Later, Romantic poets preferred run-on lines. They also favored imagination, feeling, and the discovery of knowledge through intuition—all important aspects of the modern Pagan community as well. Famous experts of the couplet form include Robert Browning, John Keats, and Phillis Wheatley.

The Alexandrine couplet characterizes French narrative and dramatic poetry. Although challenging to write in English, this meter works beautifully in French, making it ideal for magical or spiritual activities that draw on French culture. Alexandrine couplets influenced both German and Dutch poetry, so they work well for heathen traditions too. Masters of heroic couplets include John Dryden and Alexander Pope.

The couplet has a very tight, concise structure. It can handle a variety of topics and tones. While the elegiac couplet mourns, the ghazal muses. As the heroic couplet suggests, the form is a popular choice for rendering legends and myths. Given its many variations, the couplet adapts well to any magical or spiritual application.

To write a couplet, you need to think in terms of pairs. One way to do this is to brainstorm a bunch of word pairs that rhyme, then work on turning each pair into its own couplet. This works well when starting from scratch, without a specific topic in mind—the pairs that pop into your mind can suggest a direction for your poem. If you have a topic, but you're not sure what to say about it, then write down a list of words relating to your topic. Then use your rhyming dictionary to look up a mate for each word, forming rhyme pairs. You can build rhymes into lines by trying out different phrases with the rhyme words until you come up with a line that sounds good.

If you already have a clear idea of what you want to say about your topic, then write down several sentences. Use each sentence as the basis for the first line in a couplet. Examine the sentence for a good rhyme word—you may need to make the sentence a little longer or shorter to fit the couplet form you're using—and put that rhyme word at the end of its line. It's okay to break a sentence in the middle and use the last part of it as the beginning of the couplet's second line; or you can put a new, shorter sentence at the end of the second line. The end word of the first couplet determines the rhyme sound for the second line. Use your rhyming dictionary to find possible end words for the second line of your couplet.

Note also that the "pair" aspect of couplets lends itself to magical and spiritual dualities, such as "above/below" or "god/goddess." You might place one half of each duality in the first line, and the other in the second line, or give each one a complete couplet. You can bury dualities in the middle of lines, or place them at the ends if they happen to rhyme. Use synonyms or swap related dualities to create rhymes. For example, "day/night" and "dark/light" don't rhyme—but "night" and "light" do rhyme and do represent opposite conditions.

How long should your poem be? That depends on the context. Take a look at the following examples of the rhyme scheme of different couplet arrangements.

The rhyme scheme of a single couplet is:

aa

A single couplet can actually stand on its own, and is the easiest composition for people to learn "on the spot." For instance, you might cast a circle at Imbolc with a candle and this couplet:

> Hand to hand we pass the flame
> Bless this place in Brigid's name

If your circle casting begins with one or two people who already know those lines, the rest of the people present will probably have learned them by the time the candle gets passed to them.

The rhyme scheme of a couplet envelope looks like this:

aabbaa...

Four to six couplets make a good short poem, giving you enough room to say something worthwhile, without bogging down the festivities. Suppose your garden is drying out. Here is a couplet envelope praying for rain:

"Praying for Rain" by Elizabeth Barrette

Hear our voices praying for rain,
Falling on garden, field, and plain.
Hear and heed us, Mother of All:
Open up your silvery shawl.
Water the flowers, fruits, and grain.
Hear our voices praying for rain.

The frequent use of two- and three-syllable words suggests the "showery" sound of rain falling. The couplets and the use of only two rhyme sounds makes the poem very dense. Repeating the first line as the last line gives it extra punch. Open your umbrellas or prepare to get wet!

The rhyme scheme of a longer couplet poem looks like this:

aabbcc...

A poem based on couplets may be any length. Here is an excerpt from a very long poem of this type, written in heroic couplets:

"An Essay on Criticism" by Alexander Pope

A little Learning is a dang'rous Thing;
Drink deep, or taste not the Pierian Spring:

There shallow Draughts intoxicate the Brain,
And drinking largely sobers us again.

Fir'd at first Sight with what the Muse imparts,
In fearless Youth we tempt the Heights of Arts,

While from the bounded Level of our Mind,
Short Views we take, nor see the lengths behind,

But more advanc'd, behold with strange Surprize
New, distant Scenes of endless Science rise!

So pleas'd at first, the towring Alps we try,
Mount o'er the Vales, and seem to tread the Sky;

Th' Eternal Snows appear already past,
And the first Clouds and Mountains seem the last:

But those attain'd, we tremble to survey
The growing Labours of the lengthen'd Way,

Th' increasing Prospect tires our wandering Eyes,
Hills peep o'er Hills, and Alps on Alps arise!

The poet cleverly uses iambic pentameter to echo the footsteps of a wayfarer making a long hike, which supports the extended metaphor of knowledge as a journey. Pope also relies on alliteration, assonance, and consonance to bind the poem together. Consider how this excerpt would make a suitable reading at an Initiation ritual or other rite of passage.

Ballad

The *ballad* consists of four-line stanzas, called *quatrains,* in which the second and fourth lines rhyme with each other. The unrhymed lines give it a slightly looser structure than the couplet. A variation, called a *double ballad,* tightens the form, as the first and third lines also rhyme with each other. Together these two versions cover a great many classic poems and folk songs.

Ballads often feature a *refrain,* a phrase or an entire line that repeats throughout the poem. Most often, the refrain encapsulates the poem's main idea. However, many traditional ballads have nonsense refrains. Some ballads have just one refrain, usually in the fourth line of each stanza, sometimes in the second and fourth line. Others use two separate refrains that rhyme with each other. An entire stanza may be repeated, as the chorus of a song—even in ballads not meant for singing.

A strong, driving rhythm characterizes this form and gives it much of its strength. This can be any regular rhythm, but an especially popular pattern, called *ballad meter*, alternates lines of iambic tetrameter and iambic trimeter. The line lengths are usually similar, but sometimes the rhyming and nonrhyming lines differ for contrast.

Folk ballads exist in multiple variations, their original authors lost to the mists of time. Literary ballads belong to a later era and a known author, although often done in similar style. In the 16th century, people began publicizing *broadsheet ballads* by printing them on cheap pages and pinning them to walls.[4] These often featured subversive heroes such as Robin Hood and Puck. Famous experts of the ballad form include Emily Dickinson, John Keats, Sir Walter Scott, and Bob Dylan.

Though not rigidly bound by tradition, the ballad comes with a number of popular customs. It is typically a narrative poem, often told in first person. Some folk ballads praise or condemn the acts of nobles known to the author, or relay morbid details of crimes—an early form of news broadcast! Others deal with folklore, legends, and magical things, or with seasonal changes, milestones of life, and other everyday matters. The style relies less on detail than on rustic simplicity and force of imagery. It applies well to any ritual purpose.

In composing a ballad, you have several key numbers to work with: two, three, and four. The ballad form uses pairs of rhyme words, as does the couplet form, but interweaves them with other lines. Use the same techniques for finding good pairs, but now you've got more room to work with. Most European folklore uses three as a magic number: three sons, three tasks, three attempts culminating in success, and so on. This pattern appears repeatedly in traditional ballads, and works well with European-derived Pagan motifs such as "maiden, mother, crone." However, the four-line verses of a ballad also lend themselves to using four as a magic number, which can be found in Native American traditions, or in contemporary Pagan sets such as Earth, Air, Fire, Water.

Repetition also characterizes this form. You can build a ballad around one great line (make it the refrain) or one great verse (make it the chorus). For variety, you might repeat a line, but change one word each time; or repeat a verse, changing one line. A subtler trick is to repeat one key word in every verse, but always in a different position. Important phrases, especially commands, may repeat immediately: "Rise up, rise up!" If you don't want to use the ballad meter, your best line or two can also set the meter for the rest of the poem. Remember, lines one and three should have the same meter; lines two and four may have the same, or a different meter of their own.

Ballads include dialogue more often than other types of poetry do. For example, two characters can speak in alternating verses—an ideal choice for the Oak King and Holly King, or other mythic pairs. Another option is a type of call and response, in which one stanza poses a question that the next stanza answers. This technique allows you to teach in an entertaining way, such as explaining the significance of a sabbat to the audience at a public ritual.

More than other poems, a ballad relies on a sense of topical organization. The verses should flow from one to another in some logical progression: chronological, spatial, emphatic, cause-effect, problem-solution, and so on. One way to outline a ballad is to describe an event in order, and give each twist of the story its own verse. For instance, the first verse introduces the main character, the second verse poses a problem, several verses detail attempts to solve it, and the last verse gives the final resolution. Another method is to write out a list of aspects or attributes relating to your main topic, and turn each into a verse or part of a verse. It's okay to write the verses out of sequence—if you think of the last verse first, don't worry about it—just sort them into the right order when you revise your ballad.

You don't have to write a long ballad, though. You can just use the ballad stanza for one or two verses. Longer ballads make good spells, if you want to describe exactly how you wish events to unfold. Short ballads make good invocations, openings and closings, and blessings.

The rhyme scheme of a ballad looks like this:

abcbdefe...

Here is a very brief ballad about the setting sun:

"The Sea of Sunset" by Emily Dickinson

This is the land the sunset washes,
These are the banks of the Yellow Sea;
Where it rose, or whither it rushes,
These are the western mystery!

Night after night her purple traffic
Strews the landing with opal bales;
Merchantmen poise upon horizons,
Dip, and vanish with fairy sails.

The poet uses sense imagery and metaphor to paint a picture of the sunset, creating a magical atmosphere. This poem also links the sea, the direction of west, and the quality of mystery—as in contemporary Paganism. This would suit a ritual at the end of the day, or on the beach.

The rhyme scheme of a double-ballad looks like this:

ababcdcd...

This famous double ballad often appears in Pagan contexts, with the lady construed as one of the many faces of the Goddess:

"Greensleeves" by Anonymous

Alas, my love, you do me wrong,
To cast me off discourteously.
For I have loved you well and long,
Delighting in your company.

(Chorus)
Greensleeves was all my joy

Greensleeves was my delight,
Greensleeves was my heart of gold,
And who but my lady greensleeves.

Your vows you've broken, like my heart,
Oh, why did you so enrapture me?
Now I remain in a world apart
But my heart remains in captivity.

(Chorus)

I have been ready at your hand,
To grant whatever you would crave,
I have both wagered life and land,
Your love and good-will for to have.

(Chorus)

If you intend thus to disdain,
It does the more enrapture me,
And even so, I still remain
A lover in captivity.

(Chorus)

My men were clothed all in green,
And they did ever wait on thee;
All this was gallant to be seen,
And yet thou wouldst not love me.

(Chorus)

Thou couldst desire no earthly thing,
but still thou hadst it readily.
Thy music still to play and sing;
And yet thou wouldst not love me.

(Chorus)

Well, I will pray to God on high,
that thou my constancy mayst see,
And that yet once before I die,
Thou wilt vouchsafe to love me.

(Chorus)

Ah, Greensleeves, now farewell, adieu,
To God I pray to prosper thee,
For I am still thy lover true,
Come once again and love me.

(Chorus)

"Greensleeves" exists in multiple versions. The earliest surviving one dates from the 16th century, and it may not have been new then. The preceeding example is one of the modern interpretations, but earlier dialect versions remain available. Note that although the main verses rhyme *abab,* the chorus does not rhyme at all! Instead, it depends on the repetition of "Greensleeves was..." for cohesion.

As in many ballads, this one employs romantic themes. Look at all the references to "my love," "my heart of gold," "a lover," and so on. Some hints of Pagan imagery include "My men were clothed all in green," and "Thy music still to play and sing." Pagan performers often change the references "to God" into "to gods" or "the gods" instead. "Greensleeves" is a staple of bardic circles, especially at Beltane or Midsummer sabbats.

Exercises

Use the following exercises to practice the basic forms of poetry presented in this chapter. You do not need to do all of them; it's okay to pick and choose. Now that you have a better understanding of these forms, you may want to double back to some exercises in previous chapters that involve writing your own compositions.

Exercise #1: Reading Practice

Read at least three poems of each type—free verse, couplet, and ballad—from any collection or anthology. Compare and contrast the different forms as you read. Which do you like best? Why? Write about this in your journal.

Exercise #2: Writing Practice

Write at least one brief poem (up to 10 lines) in each form. You may choose whatever topics you wish, but vary the types—such as one prayer, one spell, and one song for use in ritual. Which form do you find the easiest to write? The hardest?

Exercise #3: The Form in Depth

Study one of these forms—free verse, couplet, or ballad—in depth, then write in your journal about its features and uses. What makes this form distinctive? Why do you like (or dislike) it more than the others? Who are some famous poets known for writing it? Find more historical background not mentioned in this chapter.

Exercise #4: Developing Detail

Use the journal entry from Exercise #3 to write a poem of your chosen form. Look to your notes on its history and uses for inspiration.

Exercise #5: Analyzing Free Verse

The following is an example of free verse. What literary techniques does the author use in this poem? What distinguishes this from prose? What magical or spiritual purposes might this poem serve? Write your answers in your journal.

"Smoke" by Henry David Thoreau

Light-winged Smoke! Icarian bird,
Melting thy pinions in thy upward flight;
Lark without song, and messenger of dawn,
Circling above the hamlets as thy nest;
Or else, departing dream, and shadowy form
Of midnight vision, gathering up thy skirts;
By night star-veiling, and by day
Darkening the light and blotting out the sun;
Go thou, my incense, upward from this hearth,
And ask the gods to pardon this clear flame.

Exercise #6: Expanding on Free Verse

Reread the poem "Fog" in this chapter. With that as a model, write a set of Quarter calls using metaphor and personification to represent each of the Elements or Directions as an animal. (You may want to skip ahead to Chapter Ten, which discusses openings and closings, or wait to do this exercise until after reaching that point.)

Exercise #7: Analyzing Couplets

Here is a poem based on couplet rhymes that have been combined into quatrains. Why do you think the poet arranged the lines this way? What is the meter? What other literary techniques can you find here? How might you use this poem in a sabbat, and which sabbat(s) would it suit? Write your answers in your journal.

"Summer Sun" by Robert Louis Stevenson

Great is the sun, and wide he goes
Through empty heaven without repose;
And in the blue and glowing days
More thick than rain he showers his rays.

Though closer still the blinds we pull
To keep the shady parlour cool,
Yet he will find a chink or two
To slip his golden fingers through.

The dusty attic spider-clad
He, through the keyhole, maketh glad;
And through the broken edge of tiles,
Into the laddered hay-loft smiles.

Meantime his golden face around
He bears to all the garden ground,
And sheds a warm and glittering look
Among the ivy's inmost nook.

Above the hills, along the blue,
Round the bright air with footing true,

To please the child, to paint the rose,
The gardener of the World, he goes.

Exercise #8: Traveling with Couplets

Couplets have appeared in many different cultures and times. Research some of these that interest you. Also, reread "An Essay on Criticism" in this chapter to see how the author uses extended metaphor. Now, write a long couplet poem (12 or more verses), using travel as a metaphor for something other than knowledge.

Exercise #9: Analyzing Ballads

Popular in bardic circles, this poem rhymes in ballad form, although the rhymes are stacked into eight-line stanzas. Why do the stanzas break where they do? What is the meter of this poem? What does it make you think of? How do the techniques used here relate to ballad tradition? Write your answers in your journal.

"The Song of Wandering Aengus" by W.B. Yeats

I went out to the hazel wood,
Because a fire was in my head,
And cut and peeled a hazel wand,
And hooked a berry to a thread;
And when white moths were on the wing,
And moth-like stars were flickering out,
I dropped the berry in a stream
And caught a little silver trout.

When I had laid it on the floor
I went to blow the fire a-flame,
But something rustled on the floor,
And someone called me by my name:
It had become a glimmering girl
With apple blossom in her hair
Who called me by my name and ran
And faded through the brightening air.

Though I am old with wandering
Through hollow lands and hilly lands,
I will find out where she has gone,
And kiss her lips and take her hands;
And walk among long dappled grass,
And pluck till time and times are done,
The silver apples of the moon,
The golden apples of the sun.

Exercise #10: Singing Your Heart Out

Reread "Greensleeves" in this chapter. Also look up some other traditional ballads with romantic themes. Using those for inspiration, write a ballad or double-ballad about divine love. You might have the Goddess and God adoring each other in alternate verses—or arguing!

Exercise #11: Collecting Examples

Leaf through some of your favorite sources of rituals and other magical writing. See how many examples you can find of free verse, couplet, and ballad forms. Choose at least one of each form to copy into your journal or Book of Shadows for use as role models.

Analyzing Poetic Rhythm

Rhythm defines the shape of the poem in the listener's ear. Meter is a regular type of rhythm based on a series of feet, which can be all the same kind or a mix. Poets often find themselves with several excellent lines whose meters don't match. This tends to make a potentially great poem sound awkward. When revising your poetry, you should check the rhythm and meter, and fix them if they don't work. Feedback from a first-reader helps with this process.

Here is a poem I critiqued for a friend. After that comes the analysis of its strengths and weaknesses, and how it might be improved.

"What Do You See" by C. Rainbow Wolf (1/31/06)

What do you see when you look at me?
A daft old woman where a girl used to be?
Someone stupid and fat with a weird sense of dress
Who rarely wears make-up and whose hair is a mess?
A silly old lady who acts way too free?
Just what do you see when you look at me?

What do you see when you watch me work?
A fast fingered typist or role model jerk?
A teacher creator whose skills multitask
Who loves her family and drinks herbs from a flask
Who believes in her visions and creates what she sees?
What do you see when you look at me?

What do you see when you look at me?
High priestess in robes or a druid rookie?
Do you see smiles and laughter or anguish and pain
Or someone who lives life again and again
Who bakes muffins and makes fudge and drinks
redbush tea
What do you see when you look at me?

What do you see when you look at me?
Can I tempt you to enter the realms that I see
Where crystals tell stories and faeries sing songs
And the moon's gentle glow is felt all day long
Where lessons are learned from wildlife and trees?
Can I tempt you into the world that is me?

Shall I tell you the things my mirror tells me?
What I see in myself when I look at me?
When I bypass the stereotypical roles that I've been
And I undistort images I know that I've seen
I know who I am, what I've been, where I'll be
I'll share this with you, if you'll just look at me.

Analysis

"Meter" or "rhythm" sets the tune of the poem. Stress falls in a particular pattern. Most rhyming poems have a regular meter: The stress follows the same pattern throughout. All the lines may have the same number of syllables, or a couple of numbers that alternate. If there are missing or extra syllables, it usually sounds a little awkward—though some poems shift meter a little and it works.

Let's start by counting the syllables in the first two stanzas:

What do you see when you look at me? (9 syllables)
A daft old woman where a girl used to be? (11)
Someone stupid and fat with a weird sense of dress (12)
Who rarely wears make-up and whose hair is a mess? (12)
A silly old lady who acts way too free? (11)
Just what do you see when you look at me? (10)

What do you see when you watch me work? (9)
A fast fingered typist or role model jerk? (11)
A teacher creator whose skills multitask (11)
Who loves her family and drinks herbs from a flask (11)
Who believes in her visions and creates what she sees? (13)
What do you see when you look at me? (9)

I think that some of the 11-syllable lines have the best meter:

ă sílly ŏld lády whŏ ácts wăy tŏo frée?
ă fást fingĕred týpĭst ŏr róle mŏdĕl jérk?
ă téachĕr crĕátŏr whŏse skílls mŭltĭtásk

Those lines are built mainly of three-syllable feet called amphibrachs: ˘ ´ ˘. They end with a two-syllable foot, an iamb: ˘ ´. This is a nice strong meter, but it's an odd one, not used very often. So it neatly suits the whimsical topic and tone of your poem.

Now let's look at some other lines.

What do you see when you look at me?

Great line; it matches the title. The drawback is that those one-syllable words don't clue your reader to a specific emphasis. It could be:

whát dŏ yŏu sée whĕn yŏu lóok ăt mĕ?

or

whăt dŏ yóu sĕe whĕn yóu lŏok ăt mé?

Those are just the lines that sound most promising. If the whole poem had 9-syllable lines, and some of those other lines had a more definite rhythm, your reader would quickly figure out the intended rhythm and apply it to the more flexible lines.

Now let's look at a line with awkward meter:

A daft old woman where a girl used to be?

You can't stress "a" or "to" in English; it sounds wrong. Stressing "where" isn't much better. The stress of "woman" has to fall on the first syllable. Which gives us something like this:

ă dáft ŏld wómăn whĕre ă gírl ŭsed tŏ bé?

It's okay up to the end of "woman," and then the line falls apart. See where there are three unstressed syllables together? Your tongue gets lost without a stress to stomp on, right in the middle of the line. You can have two unstressed syllables together, but three is awkward.

Here are two 12-syllable lines, one with a nice regular meter and one that stumbles:

sŏmeŏne stúpĭd ănd fát wĭth ă wéird sĕnse ŏf dréss

whŏ rárelў wĕars máke-ŭp ănd whŏse háir ĭs ă méss?

Look at the first of the pair; those are anapests: ˇ ˇ ´. This is a driving rhythm that sounds like a horse cantering. It was well written, but it probably doesn't fit this poem's mood as well as the quirky amphibrachs. Anapests usually appear in festive, political, or martial poetry, or other places where you really want a fast hammering beat that falls forward and then stomps on the end.

Now the second line is different. See those two amphibrachs at the beginning? The audience will expect this line to match the other amphibrach lines, and it doesn't. There are three un-stressed syllables in a row again: "up," "and," and "whose." The rhythm makes two good moves and then falls flat on its face.

The good thing about all of this is that there *are* several lines in perfect meter. The poet is capable of making good choices; those were probably lines that made her think, "Aha! I like that one!" The others may not have sounded quite right, but she wasn't sure why.

When you start writing a poem, think of which lines you like the very best. Try to find two or more of those that have the same meter. Then make that your meter for the poem, and make all the other lines fit that meter. (You may want to mark stresses with hash marks, as I've done here, or count syllables on your fingers.) If you write down a line that doesn't match, try rearranging the phrases, or putting in synonyms with a different syllable count, to say the same thing with the right rhythm. This just takes practice.

Chapter Five:
Making Magical Poetry—
Additional Forms

Imagine the three basic forms discussed in Chapter Four (free verse, couplet, and ballad) as primary colors. Beyond those lies a whole palette of other forms, diverse and vibrant. Familiarizing yourself with more forms allows you greater choice when you paint with words. Most poetry handbooks demonstrate half a dozen to a dozen forms, which is plenty for most poets. If you really love forms, then research online archives of form descriptions or acquire a reference such as *The Book of Forms: A Handbook of Poetics* (Third Edition) by Lewis Tresco. Some forms belong to an ethnic group, with strong ties to a particular time, place, and people. They readily evoke the mood of their home culture, and the gods of that culture will recognize its native forms and may prefer them above others. So, ethnic forms work especially well for rituals involving the tradition from which that form springs.

Other forms are more widespread, or modern in derivation. They offer more flexibility. You may find that you favor using a certain form for a certain purpose, such as acrostic poems for deity invocations, spelling the deity's name. In situations in which cultural connections would bring more disadvantage than advantage, consider using a modern or multicultural form instead. Modern forms tend to carry little or no cultural baggage. You can even design your own forms, using the basic techniques (alliteration, allusion, metaphor, and so on) and units (feet, lines, stanzas) to create something exactly suited to your needs.

The more advanced forms of poetry may or may not rhyme. The ones that rhyme often have a complicated pattern. The ones that don't rhyme are characterized by other rules that dictate their shape or content. Choose carefully, and suit the form to your needs, for these carry a distinct flavor that will influence the ritual. The additional forms detailed here are: acrostic, haiku, list poem, sonnet, and villanelle.

Acrostic

The *acrostic* derives its nature from a single rule. This type of poem works similarly to a crossword puzzle, spelling a word or phrase with certain letters of its lines.[1] This hidden message refers to the poem's topic; many acrostics take their title from the vertical content. Most often, the first letter of each line spells something down the left-hand margin. Other times, the final letters do the spelling, a variation called *telestich*. If letters in the middle of the lines are used in this manner, that's *mesostich*. When both the first and the final letters spell something, it's called a *double acrostic*.

The simplest form of acrostic poetry uses one word per line, making this a variant of the list poem (see page 107). However, it's tricky to make these sound interesting, because you have so little space. Another type of acrostic uses multiple words per line, allowing you to tell a story or describe a topic in more detail. A long poem of this type might spell a whole sentence down its margin, such as "All that you do returns to you, times three."

Traditionally, acrostic poems do not rhyme. Sometimes, though, poets write them with the rhyme pattern of a different poetic form, as added disguise for the vertical message. Readers rarely expect an acrostic when they see rhyme!

The origin of acrostic poetry is shrouded in mystery. However, we know this form must post-date the invention of writing, unlike forms based in oral tradition, because it relies on the appearance of the written word on the page. Some Greek and Latin examples survive, along with later works in German, Slavic, and Italian languages. Experts of this form include Gottfried of Strassburg, Rudolph of Ems, Boccaccio, Sir John Davies, Mistress Mary Fage, and Edgar Allen Poe.

Acrostic verses appear in different cultures, particularly in esoteric and spiritual texts. They have been used to send secret messages, or help members of an organization to identify each other. This form works well in a magical context because it contains a little secret all its own. Many people have read an acrostic poem and never noticed its hidden nature! The vertical message serves to tie the poem together very tightly. As an opening, closing, or invocation, consider spelling the name (such as "East" or "Aradia") of what you are addressing. For blessings or incantations, use the objective (such as "Heal Swiftly" or "Inspiration") as the message.

The first step in writing an acrostic is to choose the word, phrase, or sentence you intend to spell along the margin. Write in those letters (usually all capitalized) down the page. Next, think of some words starting with those letters. If you're sure you want to use a specific word, attach it to the appropriate letter and leave it in place. Otherwise, you can put a string of words on a line, all starting with the same letter, and wait until later to make up your mind. Finally, go through and "connect the dots," adding more words and phrases to complete the poem around the framework of chosen words.

Here is a sample acrostic relating to the Autumnal Equinox:

"MABON" by Elizabeth Barrette

May we pause, in the year's journey,
And reflect on our progress:
Births and deaths, joys and regrets.
Our lives, like the year, like the
Night and day, find balance.

As the title suggests, this poem spells "Mabon" down the left margin. It also uses short phrases to shape the rhythm, creating the "pause" effect mentioned in the first line. The combination of one- and two-syllable words evokes a sense of motion. Assonance repeats the long "e" of "we," "year," "journey," "reflect," and "regrets;" the short "e" of "reflect" and "progress;" and the long "i" of "lives" and "night." Altogether, the poem sounds a bit like a wagon wheel turning or a seesaw shifting position. It would make a good reading at the Autumnal Equinox.

Haiku

Haiku is a *syllabic* form of poetry, meaning that its structure relies on a certain number of syllables per line, in this case, 5-7-5. The first line has five syllables, the second line has seven, and the third has five.[2] A haiku captures a single moment in time, not a narrative flow of events—a snapshot, a flash of inspiration, an "aha!" experience. Thus, it usually appears in the present tense. The topic focuses on some aspect of nature, and traditionally includes a seasonal clue. For instance, cherry blossoms indicate spring, and bonfires indicate fall. Haiku celebrates the ordinary, using literary techniques less than other poems. Often, one line is conceptually separated from the other two, creating an interesting break or juxtaposition of different ideas. Haiku does not rhyme.

The haiku form comes from Japan. The historic haiku masters include Bashô, Buson, and Issa. In contemporary times, poets such as Jack Kerouac have used haiku to celebrate simplicity, which modern life often lacks.

Closely associated with Zen Buddhism, haiku also meshes well with other Eastern religions and magical systems, and with contemplative traditions in general. It is the poetry of paradox, calling attention to the contrary and the nonsensical, and frequently attempting to bend language in such a way as to illuminate concepts that cannot readily be expressed in words. It also stacks layers of meaning, from the everyday to the metaphysical.

These traits suit haiku to magical uses. It's an obvious choice for any activity with an Eastern theme, but also for mind magic, philosophy, enlightenment, crazy wisdom, and related concepts. Haiku works well whenever you want something short and punchy, especially for openings and closings, or situations in which numerous people each need to read something. Its concise nature also makes it ideal for written spells in which the words have to fit in a small space.

When you write haiku, think "hook, line, and sinker." The first line should grab the reader's attention. The second should elaborate or contrast an idea. The third should give the poem an emphatic close, similar to the punch line of a joke.

Make every word count! This is more important in microforms such as haiku than in longer narratives. Avoid adding words as filler just to make the syllable-count measure properly. Likewise, minimize the use of articles and prepositions, which contribute little to the poem's impact. Instead, seek concrete nouns and dynamic verbs, with a few well-chosen adverbs and adjectives. Haiku also make more use of interjections than most other poems do.

Here is one example from the famous haiku master, Bashô:

> At the ancient pond
> a frog plunges into
> the sound of water[3]

Japanese culture is fascinated with the sound of water. This poem cleverly plays on that with synaesthesia, by having the frog plunge, not into the water itself, but into the *sound* of the water splashing from the jump. The frog suggests springtime. This would make a lovely Quarter call (or dismissal) for West/Water.

List Poem

The *list poem*, also known as catalog verse, is exactly what it sounds like: a poem that names many examples (people, places, things, attributes, even abstract ideas) around a common theme.[4] Each line may be a single word, or a phrase. Often, but not always, the poet includes a brief, colorful description of each item listed. List poems based on phrases rather than one-word lines may begin each line with the same word or phrase. The poem often concludes with a surprise or twist that casts the list in a new light, and the closing line(s) may differ in structure from the rest. A list poem usually appears in free verse, but it may rhyme (usually in ballad or couplet pattern). It has a strong rhythm, which may or may not fall into a regular meter. This form belongs to the family of *didactic poetry*, used for instruction because it makes things easier to memorize.

In its simplest manifestation—a litany of names alone—this may well be the oldest form of poetry. The list poem spans languages and ages. Those long litanies of ancestors in Bible verses, and of ships in Homer's epics, are essentially list poems. Contemporary poets may draw their inspiration from laundry lists, grocery lists, or any of the dozens of other lists that are a part of modern life. Expert writers of list poetry include Homer, Gerard Manley Hopkins, Shel Silverstein, Walt Whitman, and Pamela Little.

List poems are ubiquitous in magical and spiritual texts. They can appear as any of the types of ritual poetry. They make especially fine chants or rounds because of their strong associations. Of course, you can also use them for their original purpose: study aids!

To write a list poem, begin with your topic. Write down a bunch of words or phrases relating to your topic. Look for patterns, and rearrange the order of the lines to emphasize what you find. A poem about a place might be organized spatially, similar to a tour; a poem about an object might list its attributes from the most general to the most specific. Feel the words in your mouth and listen to their sounds as you say them. If they don't flow well, substitute synonyms until you find something that works. A list poem needs especially good flow from one line to another.

Here is a list poem using one-word lines to create images of autumn:

"September Palette" by Elizabeth Barrette

amber

carmine

umber

garnet

mocha

murrey

cocoa

honey

orange

roan

ochre

lemon

saffron

russet

madder

mustard

all the colored

leaves of autumn

Written in trochees, this poem's regular meter makes it suitable for chanting. Alliteration, assonance, and consonance all tie the words together. Notice how many words sound very similar without quite rhyming perfectly. The color words are paired, but the pairs interweave: "amber" and "umber" go together, as do "carmine" and "garnet." The last two lines are trochaic dimeter instead of trochaic monometer; the change focuses attention here, where the topic of the poem is revealed. This poem lends itself well to autumn esbats or sabbats, and to any spell or ritual involving fallen leaves.

Sonnet

The *sonnet* has 14 lines. It may be written as a single stanza, or divided. It's often written as two stanzas with an octave (eight lines) and a sestet (six lines); as four stanzas with three quatrains (four lines) and a couplet (two lines); or as four stanzas with two quatrains (four lines) and two tercets (three lines).[5] The rhyme scheme also varies, as different traditions and authors express their own preferences; see pages 109–112 for some common patterns. All the rhymes are charmingly complex and tie the poem together very well. The traditional rhythm is iambic pentameter, but can vary. The poet develops a single idea throughout the poem, often with a twist or summary of the theme in the last two lines. A *sonnet sequence* presents a set of sonnets around the same foundation, such as Lady Mary Wroth's "Pamphilia to Amphilanthus."

Italy is the birthplace of the sonnet. Its first masters included Giacomo da Lentini and Petrarch. The early Petrarchan form survived despite later variations; Elizabeth Barrett Browning favored Petrarchan sonnets. Shakespeare altered the rhyme pattern, writing many sonnets in the 16th century. Edmund Spenser interlaced the rhymes, reusing them in later lines. So don't hesitate to play with this form yourself.

Many existing sonnets are ideal for use in ritual, as they often deal with classical deities, pastoral imagery, or popular spellcraft goals such as love. They create a sense of rolling grandeur, ideal for public rituals or other occasions when pageantry adds to magical or spiritual effect. This form makes terrific openings and closings, if you want something detailed but still easy to memorize; the driving beat of iambic pentameter combined with a tight rhyme scheme really pounds the phrases into your brain. For invocations, blessings, or incantations, the sonnet is a tight form that makes you target your ideas precisely. The cultural connections to Italy and England, and the sophisticated classical structure, make this a good choice for formal rituals or ones based on European traditions.

When composing a sonnet, begin with the theme, because this is foremost a poem of idea. Plan to present a conflict of some kind, with the setup in the initial stanza(s) and the resolution in the closing stanza(s). An extended metaphor provides an excellent structure for developing your theme. Simile, metonymy and synecdoche, personification, allusion, and other literary techniques (as discussed in Chapter Three) add to the ornate style of a sonnet. Don't overload the reader, but rather choose one to three techniques to showcase in a given poem.

Sonnets are traditionally written in iambic pentameter, so pay careful attention to meter as you write your lines. You may need to move words or whole phrases to accommodate the meter and the rhyme pattern. Happily, you have a choice of several rhyme patterns! So it's perfectly acceptable to write the first couplet or quatrain however seems most natural for that poem, and then map out the rest of the rhyme pattern based on that beginning—or even to write a closing and backtrack. If you get a solid *abba* quatrain to start with, then go on with the Petrarchan pattern; if you have a tight couplet conclusion, choose between Shakespearean or Spenserian patterns for the body.

The rhyme scheme of a Petrarchan/Italian sonnet looks like this:

abbaabbacdcdcd

Here is a famous sonnet written in the Petrarchan pattern:

"The World Is Too Much With Us"
by William Wordsworth

The world is too much with us; late and soon,

Getting and spending, we lay waste our powers;

Little we see in Nature that is ours;
We have given our hearts away, a sordid boon!
This Sea that bares her bosom to the moon,
The winds that will be howling at all hours,
And are up-gathered now like sleeping flowers,
For this, for everything, we are out of tune;
It moves us not. —Great God! I'd rather be
A Pagan suckled in a creed outworn;
So might I, standing on this pleasant lea,
Have glimpses that would make me less forlorn;
Have sight of Proteus rising from the sea;
Or hear old Triton blow his wreathéd horn.

Notice the way Wordsworth varies the strict iambic pentameter form in the *b* lines, with the two-syllable rhyme of "powers," "ours," and so forth. He also uses vivid sense imagery, personification, and allusion to create a potent sense of wonder at the natural world, and yet contrasts that with feelings of longing and emptiness. This sonnet might grace the initiation ritual of someone coming to Paganism after much searching and dissatisfaction on other paths.

The rhyme scheme of a Shakespearean/English sonnet looks like this:

ababcdcdefefgg

This sonnet demonstrates the Shakespearean pattern:

"Sonnet C" by William Shakespeare

Where art thou Muse that thou forget'st so long,
To speak of that which gives thee all thy might?
Spend'st thou thy fury on some worthless song,
Darkening thy power to lend base subjects light?
Return forgetful Muse, and straight redeem,
In gentle numbers time so idly spent;

Sing to the ear that doth thy lays esteem

And gives thy pen both skill and argument.

Rise, resty Muse, my love's sweet face survey,

If Time have any wrinkle graven there;

If any, be a satire to decay,

And make time's spoils despised every where.

Give my love fame faster than Time wastes life,

So thou prevent'st his scythe and crooked knife.

By turns coaxing and exasperated, this poem directly addresses the "Muse," who may be one of the nine Greek goddesses of creative expression, or the author's personal spirit of inspiration. Observe the way each of the quatrains, and the concluding couplet, addresses a different aspect of the situation. This approach works well for spells, and indeed, this sonnet would suit a spell to relieve writer's block.

The rhyme scheme of a Spenserian sonnet looks like this:

ababbcbccdcdee

Here is a sonnet in the Spenserian pattern:

"Sonnet LXXV" by Edmund Spenser

One day I wrote her name upon the strand,

But came the waves and washed it away;

Again I wrote it with a second hand,

But came the tide and made my pains his prey,

"Vain man," said she, "That dost in vain assay

A mortal thing so to immortalize,

For I myself shall like to this decay,

And eke my name be wiped out likewise."

"Not so," quod I, "Let baser thing devise

To die in dust, but you shall live by fame;

My verse your virtues rare shall eternize

And in the heavens write your glorious name,

> Where, whenas death shall all the world subdue,
> Our love shall live, and later life renew."

The conversation, with its different opinions on permanence vs. impermanence, divides the focus of the poem into two sections: an octave and a sestet. This shows the way things may be done and undone in a single poem. Also, listen to the long vowels in the rhymes: "away," "immortalize," "fame," "subdue," and so on. They make the poem seem to linger and echo, suggesting eternity through sound. This poem includes a fascinating image of writing something in the sand to be washed away—a fine magical technique for banishing. It would be possible to use this as inspiration for writing a banishment or release.

Villanelle

The *villanelle* consists of 19 lines arranged into six stanzas: five tercets (three lines) followed by a quatrain (four lines). This interlaced form repeats the lines from the opening tercet as refrains (see the following pattern).[6] Only two rhymes appear in this form. The meter is often iambic pentameter, but may be mixed, with each rhyme having a different meter. A villanelle sounds especially interesting with one feminine rhyme and one masculine rhyme, which varies the meters.

Jean Passerate invented this French form, which later spread to England and America. Other experts include Elizabeth Bishop, Edwin Arlington Robinson, Theodore Roethke, and Oscar Wilde. Dylan Thomas's villanelle "Do Not Go Gentle Into That Good Night" stands out from the crowd.

This form is well suited to service as a spell, prayer, blessing, or invocation. Adventurous bards might try the villanelle as a song. The repetition adds a great deal of emphasis, so make sure to put your main idea there. The interlacing lines create a sense of connection, weaving things together—an excellent auditory metaphor for magic.

In order to create a villanelle, you first need two great lines that rhyme. They will become your refrains. Now put another line between the first two, linking or separating them in concept. This line determines your second rhyme. Remember, this entire poem uses only two rhyme sounds, so choose them carefully! You want sounds with many rhyming words: "bay," "sphere," "night," and so on. Map out the rhyme pattern and copy your refrains into the appropriate lines. Then fill in the blanks between the refrains to complete your poem.

The rhyme scheme of a villanelle looks like this:

A(1)bA(2) abA(1) abA(2) abA(1) abA(2) abA(1)A(2)

Some poets make slight variations in the refrains as they repeat. A clever device, if applied well, is to reverse the order of the refrains in the quatrain, making the first line of the poem also its last.

Here is a sample villanelle:

"Theocritus: a Villanelle" by Oscar Wilde

O Singer of Persephone!
In the dim meadows desolate
Dost thou remember Sicily?

Still through the ivy flits the bee
Where Amaryllis lies in state;
O Singer of Persephone!

Simætha calls on Hecate
And hears the wild dogs at the gate;
Dost thou remember Sicily?

Still by the light and laughing sea
Poor Polypheme bemoans his fate:
O Singer of Persephone!

And still in boyish rivalry
Young Daphnis challenges his mate:
Dost thou remember Sicily?

Slim Lacon keeps a goat for thee,
For thee the jocund shepherds wait,
O Singer of Persephone!
Dost thou remember Sicily?

The rhetorical question gives this poem much of its haunt-
ing allure. Listen to how the meter shifts around the masculine and feminine rhymes, similar to a boat rocking. One by
one, the poet presents images characteristic of Greece and
Sicily, creating a sense of yearning and nostalgia. This poem
might appear in a spring ritual (the time of Persephone), or
another activity held in a Hellenic tradition.

Extra Forms

In addition to the forms already detailed, with instructions and examples, there are many more. Here are a few
extras, with just a brief description. You may explore these
further on your own if you wish, or investigate still others—
there are hundreds, if not thousands, of poetic forms to choose
from. You can even invent your own forms, customized to
your needs!

Conachlann

The *conachlann* dates back at least to medieval times. This
form of chain verse comes from Ireland, practiced by the bards.
The last word of each line repeats as the first word of the
following line. Often, the very last word of the poem is the
same as the very first word of the poem, tying the whole thing
together. The repetition may be exact, or may slightly vary
the form of the word, such as "gold" and "golden." The
conachlann makes an excellent chant, prayer, blessing, or
invocation. It vividly evokes an Irish or Celtic tradition.

Concrete Poetry

Concrete poetry, also called shape poetry, takes maximum
advantage of the controlled line breaks that characterize verse
in general. The poem literally takes the shape of its subject,

based on the layout of the words on the page. For example, a poem for a love spell might have a heart shape. Removing the shape would weaken or destroy the poem.

Praise Poetry

Praise poetry comes from Africa, and survives in some African-diaspora cultures worldwide. It can be performed as a song or a chant, and it relies on heavy rhythm instead of rhyme for cohesion. This is a "call-and-response" form: The poet delivers one line, and the audience delivers the next. The poet's lines are all different, but the audience's line remains the same. Each line gives an honorific title or flattering description of the person or deity who is the subject of the praise poem. This form sounds terrific in rituals, including large public ones, and is especially apt for rites of passage or invoking deities; it also suits any occasion with an African theme.

Triolet

The *triolet* has one stanza of eight lines, with two refrains. Line one repeats in lines four and seven; line two repeats in line eight. It is acceptable to make small variations in the refrains, especially in the punctuation. The rhyme scheme is:

ABaAabAB

The affect of those two refrains is relentless, making this ideal for spells or invocations. The triolet comes from 13th century France.

Waltz Wave

The *Waltz Wave* consists of one 19-line stanza. Each line has a specific number of syllables: 1, 2, 1, 2, 3, 2, 1, 2, 3, 4, 3, 2, 1, 2, 3, 2, 1, 2, 1. It's acceptable to break words into separate syllables to make them fit into the lines. The cyclic increase and decrease of syllables per line gives the poem its characteristic wavelike shape and sound. More particularly, the 2, 1, 2, 1 conclusion creates a sense of "falling away" or "diminishing." It makes this form especially apt for devocations and banishings. Yet it also has a rhythmic, soothing sound that fits a variety of gentle topics. Created by Margaret Carlisle, this contemporary form honors Leo Waltz, Manager of *Sol Magazine*.

Exercises

Use the following exercises to practice the additional forms of poetry presented in this chapter. As always, you do not need to do all of them; it's okay to pick and choose. Now that you have a better understanding of these extra forms, you may want to double back to some exercises in previous chapters that involve writing your own compositions.

Exercise #1: Expanding Your Horizons

Read at least a dozen poems, including at least three different ethnic or other advanced forms. What makes each form unique? Which do you like best, and why? Write down your thoughts in your journal.

Exercise #2: Exploring Your Roots

What magical or spiritual tradition do you practice? Where did your ancestors come from? Follow these trails back to an ethnic group or geographic region. Research what forms of poetry they used.

Exercise #3: The Acrostic Eye

Working with magic means learning to look at the world a little sideways. Write an acrostic poem using the word WITCHCRAFT for the margin, or the name of some other magical/spiritual tradition you prefer.

Exercise #4: Haiku Repair

The haiku form uses a pattern of five syllables in the first line, seven in the second, and five in the third. This haiku is intended to release the Element of Metal in an Oriental-themed ritual. Whoops—it has too many syllables! Can you fix it?

glittering metal edge

its descent describes a smooth arc

opening the circle

Exercise #5: Counting Your Blessings

The following is an excerpt of a list poem from Celtic tradition. Using this as inspiration, write a poem expressing thanks for the good things in your life.

"The Pleasant Things of Taliessin" from *The Book of Taliessin IV*

A pleasant virtue, extreme, penance to an extreme course;

Also pleasant, when God is delivering me.

Pleasant, the carousal that hinders not mental exertion;

Also pleasant, to drink together about horns.

Pleasant is Nud, the superior wolf-lord;

Also pleasant, a generous one at Candlemas tide.

Pleasant, berries in the time of harvest;

Also pleasant, wheat upon the stalk.

Pleasant, the sun moving in the firmament;

Also pleasant, the retaliators of outcries.

Pleasant, a steed with a thick mane in a tangle;

Also pleasant, crackling fuel.

Pleasant, desire, and silver fringes;

Also pleasant, the conjugal ring.

Pleasant, the eagle on the shore of the sea when it flows;

Also pleasant, sea-gulls playing.

Pleasant, a horse with gold-enamelled trappings;

Also pleasant to be holiest in a breach....

Exercise #6: Compare and Contrast

The sonnet and the villanelle are both sophisticated forms, which lend a certain rolling grandeur to their subject. How are they similar? How are they different? Write two poems, one in each form, but on the same topic. How did the form affect your handling of the subject matter? Record your findings in your journal.

Exercise #7: Further Afield

Choose one of the extra forms mentioned in this chapter. Research more about it—which poets are known for writing in that form, what its most famous examples are, its historic context, and so on. Use your findings as inspiration for writing a poem in this form.

Exercise #8: Field Trip

Attend a live poetry reading. Check your nearby bookstores, libraries, coffee shops, or universities for announcements of such events. If you still can't find one, hold a small reading with your family or friends. Do you find poetry more exciting when read aloud, or when you read silently to yourself? What do you like and dislike about a live reading? Journal your experiences.

Chapter Six:
Spinning Special Spells

What is a spell? It's the first thing that many people think of when the topic of magic comes up, but what is it, really? A *spell* is a magical composition that the caster's Will can use to reshape reality. Most spells combine words, actions, and objects to create a kind of "handle" for the Will to grasp, rather like using a wrench to tighten or loosen a nut that wouldn't yield to fingers alone. It's tempting to grab the shiny new tool and start playing with it—but wait. First you need to know what you're trying to accomplish.

Spellcraft holds great power, so approach it with respect. This is an art and science practiced by a wide diversity of Witches, wizards, magicians, and other mystical practitioners in many traditions. Know what you are about to do before you do anything. Keep records of your successes and failures, as much as possible; over time, you will learn what works for you and what does not. Choose wisely, and take responsibility for the outcome of your spellcraft.

Identify Your Goal

What drives a spell is desire. The caster's want or need provides much of the direction and power for the spell. This explains why many magical texts advise writing your own spells: Only you can know *exactly* what you want and need. Likewise, it explains the reason for casting spells yourself rather than asking someone else to do them for you: The other person might have more experience, but you have more *desire*. (If you lack experience, but your need is urgent, consider teaming up with a more advanced practitioner for a group spell.)

Thus, the first step in composing a spell is to identify your desire. This may prove more challenging than you expect. People are vastly complex creatures! You contain a glittering web of intermeshed wants and needs, from the trivial to the vital.

Imagine a spider's web. Fine, sticky strands form a spiral from the outside to the center. Those are your surface desires, the things you want, and they are the most obvious. Your attention readily "sticks" to them. But they are supported and connected by the radial lines: thicker, nonsticky cables that run from the outermost edge directly to the center. Those are your deepest and strongest desires, your needs. It's easy to get tangled up in surface desires, without ever identifying your underlying ones. The strongest spells relate to needs rather than wants, because needs connect directly to the core of your being. In order to work a spell for wants, you must identify the supporting need or needs.

Suppose you've decided to seek a new job. The first thing you think of is money; you need a good paycheck to support your family. But if you focused only on that, you might wind up with a job that has you working 60 hours a week, leaving little time for family life. Exploring deeper, you discover that you want money because you need security, which itself leads even deeper to a desire for happiness in your life. By working all of these wants and needs into your spell, you would increase your chances of finding a job that balanced a reasonable amount of pay for work you could derive some pleasure from doing, and still leave time for your family. It would probably pay somewhat less than the 60-hour-a-week job, but it would serve you better in the long run.

It takes time and practice to get to know yourself well enough to determine these things quickly and precisely. Such is the work of magical folk, across cultures and down through the ages. This practice also lends itself well to reading other people, so that when someone asks you to cast a spell for them—and people will!—you'll be able to discern whether they ask from want or need, and how you should proceed.

Say What You Mean

Magic lives in the Will, but moves through the word. For this reason, magical practitioners must take exceptional care with what they say, both in everyday life and in spellcasting. When you work magic through principles such as "As I will, so mote it be," the universe becomes accustomed to shaping itself according to your words. Thus, if you lie, or your phrasing is unclear, or you say something casually that you didn't really mean, it undermines your power. The more honest and accurate your words, the more your power grows.

Certain magical conventions have evolved from observed patterns. Specific terms tend to prove more effective than general ones, as they give the spell a tighter focus. Positive expressions ("wind, blow gently") work better than negative ones ("wind, do no harm"). Some magical theorists posit that the universe does not perceive negatives very reliably, so using them in a spell can cause it to backfire. Say what you want, not what you don't want.

A spell works similarly to a computer program, requiring the same kind of precision in order to perform properly. Writing a spell thus demands special attention to phrasing. Every word holds uncommon weight. You must say exactly what you mean, everything that you mean, and nothing that you do not mean. Unclear terms in a spell can lead to unfocused or misfired magic in the process, and undesirable side effects or spell failure in the end. Furthermore, *everything* you say in a spell will weave its way into the magic, moving toward manifestation. Don't say it if you don't want it!

Because of this, many casters use phrases that serve as "safety catches." Some are intended to prevent a magical backlash in case the spell cannot complete its objective or is otherwise interrupted, and may include a specific time limit, such as "At the end of the moon, if any energy from this spell lingers outside its goal, it shall return to the Earth, with harm to none." Others are conditional modifiers meant to avoid locking in a course that turns out not to be a good idea, such as the opening "If it be for the good of all..." Some lines maximize flexibility, allowing that forces exist who possess greater insight than any human; for instance, "Give me what I ask for, or an equivalent, or better, as the universe may provide."

The Parts of a Spell

In the broadest sense, a *spell* is the whole process by which casters use their Will to affect reality. Sometimes the term "spell" refers exclusively to the words of the spell—more properly called the *incantation*.

The three main parts of a spell are verbal (written or spoken words), active (gestures and motions), and material (tools and supplies); our concern here is with the verbal parts. Simple spells may employ just one part. For example, the children's rhyme "Rain, rain, go away, come again another day" is a spell consisting only of an incantation. Everyone knows the "cross your fingers" sign for good luck (or swearing falsely), a spell based on an action. Most spells are a complex interaction of multiple parts. Pour salt around an area to be protected, and you've got a two-part spell: pour (active), and salt (material). An old bit of folk magic goes, "Find a penny, pick it up, and all day long you'll have good luck." See how the incantation (verbal) tells you how to work the spell: When you locate a penny (material), you pick it up (active). All three parts work together.

This book primarily concerns the written word as used in magic. But keep in mind that it's hard to write a good incantation if you don't know what else will be going on in the spell. Also, the more complex the spell, the more important it is to write at least an outline of what will be happening, so you don't get lost. Finally, many incantations specifically describe the actions and objects employed in the spell process, which gives you something to put in the verbal portion, and helps tie all the components together, for a smooth and potent magical effect.

Essentially, the parts of a spell work together much the way parts of a play do: The incantation serves the same purpose as the dialog. The actions in a spell, as with those of a play, need stage directions to define and guide them. Spell materials take the role of props and setting. The caster of a group spell serves very much as a director; in a solitary spell, the caster is more similar to the single character in a one-person play. In either case, the caster must unite all the aspects of the spell to create an effective presentation.

Verbal parts of a spell include those words to be spoken aloud or written on objects during the spell. They define the spell's purpose and direct its energy in a detailed and specific way.

You must decide what kind of incantation you want, and how many. A simple spell may have one main verbal component, but a complex spell may include several incantations working together. For example, three items (each with a different power) might receive individual incantations to charge them with power, before being combined in a pouch.

When composing an incantation, first decide on the format. Writing an incantation as a poem tends to add power and cohesion, and often formality. Prose incantations can be formal or informal. Also, poetry works better for short to medium incantations, as few people have the patience to deal with really long poems. Lengthy incantations usually do bet ter in prose. Take care with the rhythm and sound of the words, whether you write in poetry or prose. The incantation should flow smoothly, so that you can read it in a commanding tone and not stumble.

For poetic incantations, review Chapters Four and Five on poetic forms. Free verse is the most casual and flexible, and still gives you good control over pacing via the line breaks. Heroic couplets or ballad verses work well in most spells, lending rhythm and rhyme. The triolet is an excellent short form for pounding in one or two ideas with great force. The sonnet lends itself especially well to ceremonial magic, and its structure tends to create a sense of progress.

For prose incantations, review Chapter Three on compo- sition techniques. Allusion, personification, alliteration, and other literary options add interest and energy. You can "hide" them in prose, binding it together and making it easier to re- member, without seeming obtrusive to the audience. Who could forget "the great grey-green, greasy Limpopo River" from Rudyard Kipling's "The Elephant's Child" fable? Listen to the repetition of "gr" and the vowels in "great, grey," and "green, greasy." A few vivid phrases in your incantation serve as step- ping stones to get you through it.

A good approach is to begin by writing out what you want in plain speech. Lay out your desire, what you want to ac- complish, and how. Then examine every word and phrase to weigh whether it says precisely what you wish, or should be replaced with something else. Use your dictionary to double- check meanings, and your thesaurus to find synonyms as necessary. Finally, add any safety catches that seem prudent to you.

Spell Topics

There are many different types of spells, divisible by topic and style. In order to do a good job of composition, you need to know what type of spell you want to cast, and then make sure everything matches it. Look up correspondences, such as those for colors, stones, and plants, in a guide such as Kerri Connor's *The Pocket Spell Creator*.

First, consider the topic. Although the number of possible topics is vast, certain ones appear often enough to develop some recognizable traits of their own. Spell topics comprise several large categories. There are many variations within a category, and other topics that fall outside of these, but the following are issues that come up for most casters sooner or later.

Communication

Communication spells deal in information. They cover such things as conversation, divination, inspiration, and telepathy. The verbal component is especially important. Special tools such as a Tarot deck make divination much easier, and framing divination inside a spell makes it more effective. Useful colors for communication spells are yellow and blue. Useful stones are azurite, celestite, sapphire, topaz, and turquoise. Useful plants are amber, honeysuckle, lemon, and spearmint are good.

Change

Change spans all kinds of motion, internal and external: transformation, personal growth, travel, and so on. Such spells often rely on gestures and actions. They also work well with lunar magic—in any phase. Useful colors for change spells are indigo, magenta, and purple. Useful stones are: alexandrite, geode, and moonstone. Useful plants are: clove, myrrh, and willow.

Healing

Healing affects both the body and the mind regarding health maintenance, longevity, recovery from illness or injury, tranquility, and the like. These spells tend to balance the different components. Poppets and herbs are often used. Useful colors for healing spells are green, blue, and pink. Useful stones are:

amethyst, aventurine, celestite, malachite, rose quartz, and sodalite. Useful plants are: bay laurel, gardenia, honeysuckle, patchouli, sage, thyme, witch hazel, and yarrow.

Love

Love spells relate to matters of family, fertility, friendship, and romance. They often include benevolent bindings and other sympathetic magic, and they benefit from a waxing or full moon. Useful colors for love spells are red, orange, and pink. Useful stones are: agate, carnelian, diamond, geode, lapis lazuli, and rose quartz. Useful plants are: clove, gardenia, nutmeg, orange, and rose.

Protection

Protection can be active or passive, and concerns such things as banishing, binding, purification, and warding. Such spells benefit from a waning or dark moon. Talismans are popular here. Useful colors for protection are black, white, red, and brown. Useful stones are: aquamarine, carnelian, diamond, garnet, hematite, onyx, and turquoise. Useful plants are: bay laurel, dragon's blood, holly, rose, and yarrow.

Success

Success spells are attractive, drawing such things as courage, justice, luck, prosperity, security, and strength. They benefit from a waxing or full moon. Useful colors for success spells are red, green, gold, and purple. Useful stones are: aventurine, bloodstone, chrysoprase, jade, opal, and tigerseye. Useful plants are: bay laurel, cinnamon, clover, and ginger.

Composing Spells

Spell design follows the same steps outlined in earlier chapters. (By this point you should be familiar with general writing skills, so these later chapters focus on what you need for a specific type of writing, and the composition sections are more concise.) However, now you're handling more than just words. You need to account for the incantation itself, the actions you will perform, and any objects used.

When writing a complex composition, you have a choice as to the order. You may compose the whole spell in sequence, from beginning to end. This often makes for a smoother flow, but it can get you stuck partway through if you don't have a clear end in mind. You may write the outline first and then the incantation. This maximizes your planning opportunity, but can leave you with words or concepts that are awkward to fit into the incantation. You may write the incantation first and then build the rest of the spell around it. This tends to make a strong incantation, and it's not hard to write directions for whatever materials or actions it mentions; but it doesn't set you up with things to put into the incantation, so make sure you don't run out of inspiration here. Try different approaches to see which works best for you. Also trust your instincts—if you get a very strong idea for one part of the spell, write it out before you forget it.

Typically, you should start by determining the topic of your spell. That's usually what prompts you to do magic in the first place, unless you just want the practice. Choose a style that suits your topic and your available resources. Some stylistic choices are entirely up to you, such as high or low magic. Others depend more on outside factors, such as whether you can find a few friends for a group spell, or have only yourself for a solitary spell.

Next, determine what symbols and correspondences to use. Look in your reference books for ideas on which gestures, herbs, stones, colors, runes, oils, incense, and such might provide assistance. Explore specific material guides such as *Aromatherapy for Healing the Spirit* and general guides such as *Holland's Grimoire of Magickal Correspondences*. Also consider what things you find personally meaningful; these can prove more effective than associations drawn from a book. If hematite works more as a power source than a grounding stone for you, go ahead and use it in energy-boosting spells.

Gradually shape a beginning, middle, and end for your casting. Figure out where you want the incantation(s) to go, when you will perform the action(s), and what you will do with the material(s). Remember that, although it is possible to do quick magic with neither altar nor protective circle, they provide valuable support when available. It is better to use them when you can, especially for novice to intermediate practitioners. These things require careful attention at the beginning of a spell, and their dismantling clearly signals the end.

You should wind up with an outline of what you will need and what you will be doing. It can be as simple or elaborate as you feel comfortable using. Outlines for brief spells may take just a few lines. Outlines for longer spells may resemble a script for a play, or an outline for a speech.

Spell design involves more complexity than the one-piece compositions presented earlier in this book. However, a spell breaks down into individual parts, which you can approach one at at time before combining them. It uses much the same resources and skills that you've already practiced. If you feel overwhelmed, just remember to take it one step at a time, and it will come together just fine.

Exercises

Practice spellcraft design through the following exercises. It is not required for you to do all of them; you may pick and choose. If necessary, refer back to earlier chapters for ideas on literary techniques and poetic forms for doing these exercises, or double back to exercises in Chapters Three, Four, and Five.

Exercise #1: Wants and Needs

Meditate on your desires for at least 10 minutes. Afterward, write down three things that you want, and three things that you need. Examine each item on your list, making sure you have identified your true goal, as discussed in this chapter.

Exercise #2: Refine Your Meaning

Choose one of the items from Exercise #1. Elaborate on your desire, framing it as precisely as possible. Use positive terms. Include a safety catch suited for the goal.

Exercise #3: Power Sources

Choose a different item from Exercise #1. With it in mind, review the methods of empowering your words. Which of those methods best suits your chosen goal? If you don't think any of them fit, devise another one that would work better.

Exercise #4: Parts of the Whole

Which part of a spell most interests you—verbal, active, or material? In your journal, write about each part, what you like about it, and what you don't. Explain how they work together in your mind.

Exercise #5: Get Set

Assemble a set of five to seven items useful for casting spells. You could choose from things mentioned in this chapter, such as a set of magical stones. Alternatively, invent a new set—if you often do bindings, for example, you might gather balls of yarn or skeins of embroidery floss.

Exercise #6: Sorting Spell Ideas

Return to your list from Exercise #1. For each item, describe what type of spell it would be. You may combine types—for instance, a fire/love spell.

Exercise #7: Poetry and Prose

Read the entry on "Sample Spells" on page 130 and compare the two brief spells therein. The "Safe Travel Spell" is written in poetry. Using the correspondences provided, or others of your own discovery, write a version of this spell in prose. The "New Job Spell" is written in prose. Design one in poetry, again using the available correspondences or additional ones. Which do you find easier to write, prose spells or poetry spells? Which do you think would work better for you?

Exercise #8: Filling in the Blanks

Read the "Rejampering Spell" in the sample section. Notice that it includes a suggestion for saying a blessing, but no words. Write your own words for this spell, either a blessing as suggested (instructions for blessings appear in Chapter Nine) or an incantation as described in this chapter.

Exercise #9: Blending Ideas

Read the "Rejampering Spell" in the sample section. More elaborate than the two simple spells you examined earlier, this one combines two themes—rejuvenation and pampering—into a single spell. Using this for inspiration, compose a spell of your own that blends two separate ideas, such as two themes or two magical elements.

Sample Spells

First, define the objective for your spell. Next, use the skills you learned in Chapter Two to brainstorm and research correspondences and other components that relate to your objective. Make a list of those for inspiration while composing your spell. Then write out the spell itself. Here are two examples, one spell written in poetry and one in prose.

"Safe Travel Spell" by Elizabeth Barrette

Objective: Enchant your car to travel safely.

Themes: Protection, travel.

Colors: Black (protection), white (protection), yellow (travel).

Herbs: Bay, cinnamon, elder, juniper, lavender, mint, oak, pepper, rose, sage, witch hazel (protection); comfrey root (safe travel), feverfew (protects travelers).

Oils and incense: Dragon's blood, frankincense (protection); "Safe Travel" hoodoo oil; sandalwood (travel).

Stones: Agate, chalcedony, citrine, garnet, jasper, lepidolite, onyx, sunstone, turquoise (protection); malachite (protects travelers); yellow carnelian (travel).

Symbols: Raido rune (travel), pentacle (protection).

Timing: Monday (travel), full moon (protection).

From these possibilities, you decide to make a charm from yellow cloth, marked with the Raido rune in black, which you'll keep in the glove compartment. The charm contains bay leaf, comfrey root, dragon's blood, and malachite. For the words of the spell, you come up with:

With these words I start my spell:
Monday morning, all is well.
Cloth of yellow holds the charm
That will ward against all harm.
Raido guards the journey-way,
Holding accidents at bay.
Comfrey root and malachite
Close this car in shields of light,
Iron-strong but bubble-thin
Keeping safe all those within.
Dragon's blood of ancient fame
Gives the gas a steady flame,
Keeps the tires turning true,
All bits doing what they do,

And the engine running well—
With these words I end my spell.

"New Job Spell" by Elizabeth Barrette

Objective: Get a great new job.

Themes: Happiness, prosperity, success.

Colors: Gold (success and employment), green (money), indigo (change).

Herbs: Catnip, meadowsweet, saffron (happiness); almond, bamboo, strawberry leaves (prosperity); ginger, lemon balm, rowan (success).

Oils and incense: Camellia, honeysuckle, patchouli (prosperity); bergamot (happiness and prosperity); cinnamon (success and removal of obstacles).

Stones: Amethyst, rose quartz, sunstone (happiness); jade, lapis lazuli, tigereye, (prosperity), amazonite, malachite (success).

Symbols: Smiley face (happiness), dollar sign (prosperity), Fehu rune (success, happiness, earned income).

Timing: Sunday (wealth), waxing crescent moon (new beginnings, increase).

You want this spell to work unobtrusively in public. During interviews, you'll wear your golden-yellow suitcoat and a dab of bergamot oil. Whenever you do anything related to your job search, you'll say (or think) the words of the spell:

I am a person of power. My power fills me with golden light, shining to guide my way. I am skilled in my work. My skills speak for my value as an employee. I am strong in my Will. My Will attracts the perfect job for me. Through this job, I find joy and success, and plenty of wealth to support my family. I send my need through this spell, and the universe responds to meet it, as water rushes to fill a hollow. For the good of all, so mote it be.

"Rejampering Spell" (Rejuvenation + Pampering) by Susan "Moonwriter" Pesznecker

Objective: Craft a solitary spell that spans hours to days and works as a personal "retreat."

Themes: Relaxation, stress release, recharging, strengthening, enhancement of well-being, peacefulness.

Colors: Blue (healing, protection, peace), brown (stability), green (healing), orange (health), white (purity), yellow (vigor, energy).

Herbs, oils, and incense: aloe, anise, basil, carnation, chamomile, clove, cumin, curry, dill, dragon's blood, eucalyptus, fennel, fern, flax, frankincense, ginseng, ivy, juniper, onion, parsley, pepper, peppermint, sage, thyme, violet, sweetgrass, witch hazel (protection; removing negative energy); allspice, apple, barley, cedar, cinnamon, fennel, garlic, horehound, mint, mugwort, nettle, rose, saffron, wood sorrel, willow (healing); caraway, celery, grape, mustard, summer savory, sweetgrass (mental strengthening); lavender, morning glory, olive, passion flower, pennyroyal, vervain, violet (peacefulness); bay, saffron, St. John's wort, sweet pea, tea (*Camilla sinensis)*, thistle (strengthening and energizing).

Stones: hematite, moonstone, obsidian, salt (grounding); amethyst, yellow zircon (happiness); amber, bloodstone, garnet, jade, jasper, lapis lazuli, petrified wood, sodalite, turquoise, red zircon (healing); aquamarine, carnelian, lepidolite, malachite, sapphire, blue tourmaline (peacefulness); agate, beryl, calcite, garnet, selenite, sunstone, tigereye, red tourmaline (strengthening).

Symbols: pentacle (protection), caduceus (health), circle (life cycles, continuity); personal sigil.

Timing: Any time from dusk (emphasizing magickal transformations) to dawn (new beginnings); Tuesday (strength, courage), Saturday (protection), or Sunday (divine power); full moon (to emphasize strengthening and empowering) or dark moon (to focus on inner quiet).

Explanation: Most of us have busy, stress-filled lives. This spell allows you to withdraw from the hectic world, look inward, and reenergize.

Start by setting the date and time for your rejampering. Allow at least two to three hours, but feel free to make an overnight or even a weekend out of it.

Next, make a "soft" plan for your rejampering. You might begin with meditation, move on to some sort of magickal study or craft, carry out spellwork, and then finish with an infused, candlelit bath. The components are up to you—here are examples of each of the previous suggestions.

o For the meditation, sit in a quiet space, dim the lights, and light a blue candle, dressed with olive oil. If desired, burn clove or dragon's blood incense. Ground, center, and then spend 10 to 20 minutes looking inward and contemplating the purpose for rejampering. Ground when finished.

o Use the period of study or craft time to tackle a new magickal project or to finish one you never quite have time for. This would be an excellent time for divination work, toolcraft, needlework, and so on.

o For the spell, perform an elemental protection ceremony. Arrange an altar with a sprig of protective herbs (chosen from the preceeding list;

tie with a blue ribbon), a small bowl of saltwater, and a thurible with smudge stick (sage, sweetgrass, and/or cedar). Circle the altar with a ring of stones (chosen from the preceeding list). Ground and center. Dip fingers into the saltwater and use to anoint your chakra points. Use the smudge to waft smoke over your body, from head to toe. As you work, imagine the stress and fatigue being cast away, and feel strength and protection covering you like a soft, invulnerable cloak. Offer a simple blessing of thanks. Use saltwater and smudge to anoint the herbal sprig, then mount it above the bedroom door as a protective amulet. Ground, center, offer thanks, and enjoy a favorite snack (dark chocolate recommended for its magickal flavonoids!).

o For the bath, draw a hot tub of water, stirring in a handful of sea salt and several drops of rosemary essential oil. Light white candles. Play soft music if desired. Ease into the tub and soak; be aware of your muscles unwinding, your thoughts easing. Use a bar of frankincense soap to wash away impurities, and imagine that the waters are cloaking you with fresh, powerful energies. When done, towel off and slip into a soft bathrobe or jammies (washed and dried in advance with a few drops of juniper essential oil added to the wash water).

o Create your own plans to fit your own time, place, and needs, then carry out the rejampering. Rejoice in the experience, and make sure to journal about it afterwards. Many blessings!

Chapter Seven: Creating Colorful Chants

Among the most famous of magical terms is *enchantment*. As the name suggests, this involves gathering and directing power through the focused use of sound. To "en-chant" something means to chant your energy and intent into it, whether the object is a person, item, ritual, or whatever. Here we will explore what chants are, how they work, how to use them effectively, and how to create them.

Historic and Mystic Uses

Many cultures have used chants, throughout time and around the world, for various purposes. Most religious and magical traditions include chanting in some form. Chants evolve over time, but some very old ones remain in use today.

Tribal cultures are especially fond of chants. African chants contributed to the roots of contemporary African-American music and Afro-Caribbean religions. The call-and-response pattern has long been popular in these cultures, creating a kind of dialog between a performer and an audience. Native American uses included group chants to accompany certain dances, and private chants to create magical effects such as invisibility or for prayer.

Hindu chants—variously called *kirtan, bhajan,* or *mantras*—form an important part of Hatha and Tantric Yoga.[1] These Sanskrit chants include words, phrases, and the names of important deities. The sounds of Hindu chants are intended to align both the chanter and the listener with divine energy. They also appear in religious ceremonies designed to attract prosperity or ward off danger.

Buddhists use chants both in monastic and private practice. They chant to prepare the mind for meditation, to invoke deities, or to instill in themselves certain virtues named in the chant. These chants often consist of short statements, lists of attributes, or other goals. The simplest is among the most famous: *om*.

Jewish and Byzantine religious chants led to the rise of Christian ones, most famously the Gregorian chants of the Middle Ages. Up to this time, the standard was *monophonic* or plainchant: one melody without either harmony or musical accompaniment. Sometime during the 9th century, *polyphonic* chants emerged.[2] They started with two melodic lines performed simultaneously at parallel intervals. Later came melodic lines that would actually cross over each other.

Contemporary Pagan chants draw on the entire musical history of chanting. They may be performed by one person or several, with the same melody or with melody and harmony. Musical accompaniment is common but not universal, including guitars, drums, harps, and other instruments. Many people learn Pagan chants through oral tradition, hearing them performed live at rituals. However, numerous books and albums of such chants exist, allowing other opportunities, such as *The Pagan's Muse* by Jane Raeburn and *A Dream Whose Time Is Coming*, by the Assembly of the Sacred Wheel and friends.

Raising and Directing Power

Chanting remains in use today among many different religions as a means of raising and directing power. In Pagan traditions, it is used both in magical spells and in celebratory rituals. The specific application tends to depend on the desired effect.

The act of chanting influences the mind. First, it gives the rational part of the mind something to do, thus keeping it out of the way so that the intuitive part of the mind can go to work.

The regular rhythm also helps the rational mind to relax and let go, while energizing the intuitive mind. With time, the repetition builds up, not just raising energy, but creating profoundly altered states of consciousness. This is why some cultures have chants that are traditionally performed for hours at a time. Other chants may be repeated only a few times, for a milder effect.

For a solitary practitioner, chanting helps create a mystical mood even in the absence of other participants or fancy trappings. Some choose to chant during their magical or spiritual workings. Others prefer to play prerecorded chanting in the background while they work. For the latter, you may use commercial chants from your favorite tradition—but you can also record your own original chants for replay during spells or rituals.

For a group of practitioners, chant unifies the intent of everyone present, creating a group mind out of the individual minds. African-style chants with a call-and-response pattern emphasize the division and the interaction between a performer and an audience, ideally suited for large public rituals or occasions when a highly respected leader is visiting a local group. Chants that combine a melodic line with a contrasting harmonic line work best in musically talented groups. Such chants evoke the complexity of different natural cycles, human and divine interactions, and so forth. Chants that use a single melodic line may be performed by one person, or by many people in chorus. Getting a whole group of people chanting together is very powerful. It facilitates a tight mental focus, as everyone does the same thing at the same time.

When working with material items, chanting provides a method of energy manipulation. The chant raises power through rhythm and repetition, then channels it into the recipient. Altar tools, spell components, and sacred spaces are often charged with power in this manner. A person can also become the recipient of a chant, as in some healing rituals. In a group context, large subjects usually sit in the center of the group; small ones may do the same, or may be passed from hand to hand during the chant. Alternatively, people may circle or spiral around the subject, adding the energy of their motion to that of the chant itself: clockwise for attraction, counterclockwise for banishing.

The performance of the chant is what shapes the process of raising, directing, and releasing energy in this context. A complex spell or ritual may incorporate several chants, each of which plays a different role—one to generate power, a different one to guide it, and another to send it on its way. However, the same effects can be achieved with a single chant by varying its intensity. Start chanting softly and slowly, perhaps with just one voice. Gradually increase the speed and volume to build energy and focus it on the subject. It takes practice to perceive this accumulation of energy and to sense the exact right moment to release it. To send off the power, raise the tempo and volume of the chant to a peak and then stop suddenly—many people add a gesture here, flinging their hands up to send off energy, or down to direct it into a specific object.

Analyzing Chants

A chant is a brief magical composition, customarily delivered partway between singing and speaking, although it can be sung or spoken normally. If performed by multiple people at the same time, they all perform the chant together in the same way. (Matters of melody and harmony concern musical composition, rather than verbal, and thus lie outside the scope of this book.) A round is a special type of chant, subdivided into two or more parts, and the performers are also subdivided. One group of performers begins the chant, and when they reach the second part of the chant, the second group of performers begins the first part of the chant. This process continues until all groups have entered the chant. The voices overlap, creating the round effect.

When it comes to magical compositions, a chant is the ultimate exchange of quality over quantity. An effective chant can be as short as one syllable! Om is a perfect example, often performed in this manner, although it also exists in a longer form: *Om mani padme hum,* which means "the jewel in the heart of the lotus." A sample of 30 Pagan chants revealed an average of 25 words per chant. The lengths also tended to cluster into short (12 to 16 words), medium (20 to 36 words), and long (50 to 65 words) ranges.

Another key feature of chants is repetition. Sounds repeat through alliteration, assonance, consonance, and rhyme, as discussed in Chapter Three. Not all chants rhyme, but many do. Words, phrases, and whole lines may also recur. When composing a chant, consider the "magic number" of your tradition as a basis for repetitions. In a Celtic context, things tend to appear in sets of three; in a Native American context, sets of four; and so on.

All chants rely on a strong rhythm. If the rhythm doesn't carry performers through the chant, they will stumble over parts of it. One good line can give you the metrical pattern for a whole chant. However, you can also vary the meter with some short and long lines, either alternating or in sets.

These main features—brevity, repetition, and rhythm—facilitate both condensation of energy and ease of learning. Ideally, listeners should be able to learn a chant after hearing it just a few times. This makes chants more useful than longer types of ritual composition for situations in which not everyone has time to study the ritual text in advance, but they need a chance to participate.

Some forms lend themselves especially well to chants. Free verse or prose style chants rely on alliteration, refrains, and rhythm more than rhyme for cohesion. They may even include one or two rhymes, a subtler effect than those with rhymes at all the line ends. Here is a chant suitable for group performance on the way to an underground ritual site:

"Down to the Cave" by Elizabeth Barrette

We go down to the cave
Bravely climbing, gravely chanting

> We go down, we go down
> Earth swallows us, water wets us
> Magic awaits us
> Down in the cave.

This chant uses sense imagery—"climbing," "chanting," "swallows," "wets," and so on—to draw in the audience. Sounds echo with the "w" in "we," "down," "swallows," "water," "wets," and "awaits"; and the "ave" in "cave," "bravely," "gravely." The phrase "We go down" also recurs, suggesting the repetitive nature of climbing itself. Parallel phrases appear in "Bravely climbing, gravely chanting;" and "Earth swallows us, water wets us / Magic awaits us." The rhythm changes as the lines vary between short and long—this is a slow, methodical chant that descends toward calm, rather than an energetic one that builds to a high pitch. Thus it helps the chanters make the spiritual descent into ritual space.

One or two couplet verses, or a single ballad verse, give a good length and rhyme structure. For example, consider the traditional rain chant:

> Rain, rain, go away
> Come again another day!

Listen to the repetition of "r" and "ay." The chant itself sounds like rain. It's so simple and catchy, you'll hear children spontaneously burst out with it whenever a sudden shower threatens a parade or other outdoor activity. And it works, if people pour enough energy into it.

List poems hang together because of categorical associations, preferably enhanced with repeated sounds. The "Waltz Wave" is a single long verse, but the syllabic count keeps it in the size range for a chant, while also creating a wave-like pattern in the rhythm. The following poem combines elements of both: a list of goddess names in Waltz Wave format.

"Calling All Goddesses" by Elizabeth Barrette

Frigg
Flora
Maeve
Venus
Morrigan
Durga
Brede
Pele
Cerridwen
Erishkegal
Hestia
Kuan Yin
Sif
We call
on You by
all Your
names—
Goddess,
come!

Although it does not have a regular pattern of rhymes, there are a few hidden ones, such as "Cerridwen" and "Kuan Yin," or "call" and "all." Other repeated sounds include the "f" in "Frigg" and "Flora," the "v" in "Maeve" and "Venus," the "g" in "Morrigan" and "Durga," and so on. This chant would serve equally well whether performed once or several times to raise power for Goddess workings. Note also that it's easy to customize by substituting the names of your favorite goddesses.

Many chants do not follow an established form, but rather devise a unique pattern of rhyme and rhythm, as in this historic chant:

"Strike It Up Tabor" by Thomas Weelkes

Strike it up Tabor and pipe us a favour,
thou shalt be well paid for thy labour:
I mean to spend my shoesole to dance about the

> Maypole,
> I will be blithe and brisk, leap and skip, hop and trip,
> turn about in the rout,
> until very weary joints can scarce frisk.

The rhythm of this chant does, in fact, "hop and trip," changing from line to line in a manner that suggests a whimsical Beltane dance. It makes frequent use of interior rhymes and near-rhymes: "tabor," "favour," and "labor"; "shoesole" and "Maypole"; "skip" and "trip"; "about" and "rout"; then "frisk" matching back up to "brisk." Consonance also appears in the end sounds: "p" in "up," "pipe," "leap," "skip," "hop," and "trip"; "t" in "it," "shalt," "about," and "rout." It's long for a chant, at 52 words, so it's not the easiest to memorize, but a solo performer could give Maypole dancers something to frisk to. The holiday references, consistent throughout, make this a terrific festival chant.

Another flexible option is call-and-response, especially popular in African-based traditions. Lines for the performer and/or the lines for the audience may rhyme, or the chant may be unrhymed. This example rhymes the audience lines:

"Come, Whirlwind Mama" by Elizabeth Barrette

[Performer] Come, Whirlwind Mama
[Audience] Thus do we call
[Performer] Oya of the storms
[Audience] So say we all

This chant has a "whirling" rhythm created by strong initial stress in each line, followed by unstressed or lightly stressed syllables in the rest of the line. The initial stress acts as a "kick" to spin the chant along to the next line's initial stress. Also, the performer names the one being called, while the audience tends the collective actions—an effective division of labor that supports the form.

Rounds offer more challenge than ordinary chants, both for the writer and the performers. But the overlay of different words and voices creates a whole new level of interest. Each verse marks a separate voice. Here is a Beltane round:

"Come Let Us All A-Maying Go"

Come let us all a-maying go,
and lightly trip it to and fro.

The bells shall ring, the bells shall ring,
and the cuckoo, the cuckoo, the cuckoo sing;

the drums shall beat, the fife shall play,
and so we'll spend our time away.

Repetition of phrases makes it easier to remember the lines, and each pair of lines has its own rhyme too. Sense imagery engages the performers with motion ("trip it to and fro") and sound ("bells shall ring"). This would suit a Beltane celebration full of music, dancing, and exuberant young people.

Composing Chants

Composing a chant is all about creating the right sound. The meaning of the words matters, of course, but the effectiveness depends more on how the words feel in your mouth and sound in your ears.

To compose a free verse or prose-style chant, start by writing your topic at the top of the page. Then write about that topic in sentences or even just phrases. What does it mean to you? What do you hope to accomplish with it? What associations come to mind? Jot all those down. Research or freewriting may help you generate this raw material.

Now refine what you have. Look for one or two sentences, or several phrases, that best capture your intent. Identify the pattern of stresses. Can you turn it into a regular meter? English naturally tends to fall into iambic stress. Check for repeating sounds. Do any of the words happen to rhyme or alliterate? If not, can you think of some synonyms that would? Pick a line or phrase and repeat it two or three times. Does it make the chant stronger, or just longer? Examine your word choice. Use active verbs and vivid nouns as much as possible;

be specific rather than general. Your dictionary and thesaurus can help you find replacements for weak words. In a chant, you don't need to follow ordinary grammar as rigidly as usual. Delete prepositions, conjunctions, and other little words if they get in the way.

Read your composition out loud as you continue to polish it. The sound should get smoother and more compelling as you go along. A chant is ready for use when reading it on the page makes you want to say it out loud, over and over, and when the sound of it builds up a hum of energy.

To compose a chant based on a poetic form, start with the topic and the rules for your form. Then do some research. List words that relate to your topic: colors, stones, names of deities, magical times, actions and ideas, and such. Alphabetize the words to find alliteration and assonance. Sort them by syllable count or stress pattern.

Next, assemble phrases using the words you've listed. Mix and match; move things around. See if some phrases naturally point to others. Fit them into the form you've chosen, then connect them with additional words as needed. Only put one or two ideas per line—you can see in the previous sample chants how that works. Repeating a great line is preferable to making up a mediocre line if you run out of ideas before you run out of room in the form.

Revising this type of chant is a little harder, because you have to stick to that form. Still, seek ways to improve your first draft. Read it out loud. Did you accidentally write a tongue twister? If so, substitute words that are easier to pronounce. Does the meter sound natural or forced? Move or change words if necessary. Use a rhyming dictionary to help with rhymes. However, you don't need to obsess over perfect rhymes unless you just want to—near rhymes work quite well in a chant.

Finally, check your revised version against the rules for the form. You may find structural errors creeping in due to changes. You can either fix those to match the form, or abandon the form and stick with the chant as written.

To compose a call-and-response chant, focus on polarity. Begin by writing "performer" and "audience," or other terms you prefer, at the top of a page. Then brainstorm for words and phrases relating to your topic, sorting them as you go into the two columns. Next, start a new page, writing "performer" and "audience" alternately down the left-hand side for as many lines as you wish the composition to have. Look at your brainstorming page and pick out your favorite words and phrases. Jot those down on the appropriate lines of your new page. Flesh out those fragments into complete lines, adding words as necessary.

Last, revise to make your call-and-response chant sound like a conversation or exchange. You may need to rearrange the order of lines, or change a few words to make the lines "weave" together properly. Get a friend's help to polish this one, if you can, as more problems will become noticable when you read the lines out loud alternately, as intended.

If you work better in audio than visual mode, there's another technique you can try. Instead of composing a chant on paper or computer screen, compose it out loud. Find a place where you won't be disturbed (you do not want an audience for this) and just start talking to yourself about your topic. Talk a little faster than your normal conversational speed; you need to build up momentum.

When you hear a catchy word or phrase, repeat it a few times so it will stick in your mind. Sound out other words that use the same consonants or vowels. Walk around, and speak with the stresses of the words matching your footsteps. Leave out words that don't sound right; only repeat the ones that make you want to say them again.

Gradually the right phrases will emerge, forming a complete chant. It's a bit like polishing rocks—the rough parts get worn away, leaving a beautiful jewel. When satisfied with the results, record your chant in audio format or write down the words.

Chants can play many different roles. By themselves, they aid meditation and other mental tasks. However, they are especially useful as components within a complex spell or ritual. Experiment with various types of chants to see which you find most effective.

Exercises

Use the following exercises to practice composing chants. It is not required to do all of them; pick and choose if you wish. You may want to go back and do some exercises in previous chapters that you skipped, or redo some with chants that you previously did with a different type of writing. Try fitting chants into a spell, as mentioned in Chapter Six. Because chants are so short, also consider doing some of these exercises more than once.

Exercise #1: Making History

Research the use of chants in your own magical or spiritual tradition, or your ethnic heritage. Find out what kinds of chants were used and how. Then write one of your own in the same style.

Exercise #2: Chants in Spellcraft

Practice using chants in a spell so that you learn how they influence the flow of energy. Memorize at least two chants: a slow, meditative one and a fast, energetic one. Design a spell in which you will use these chants, and compare how they sound and feel when you perform them. Afterward, write about the experience in your journal.

Exercise #3: Examining Chants

Study the following chant. What characteristics can you identify? How might you use this chant in a magical or spiritual context? Journal your thoughts.

"Africa" by William Billings

Now shall my inward joy arise,
And burst into a song;

Almighty Love inspires my heart;
and Pleasure tunes my tongue.

Exercise #4: Listening to Chants

Browse the recommended resources in this book for ideas, and listen to some recorded chants. If possible, attend a festival or other event where you can hear chants performed live. What chants did you listen to? How were they used? Were you able to learn any new chants by listening to them? Write about your experiences in your journal.

Exercise #5: Calling All Gods

Reread the chant "Calling All Goddesses" earlier in this chapter. Using either the Waltz Wave or list form, or a combination of both, write a chant based on the names of gods.

Exercise #6: Round and Round

This round is written for four voices, and it talks about traveling between worlds. Using this for inspiration, write a round about the Faerie world.

"Hey We to the Other World"
Hey we to the other world lads
where tis thought they very merry be;
there the Man in the Moon drinks Claret;
a health to thee to me.

Exercise #7: Free Chant

Choose a magical topic such as healing, prosperity, or success. Compose a free verse or prose-style chant with a slow, meditative tone to focus your inner self on this topic.

Exercise #8: Correspondence Chant

Pick a magical time, such as a moon phase or time of day, and a rhymed, metered form of poetry. Research the correspondences for your topic, and look up the rules for your form. Then compose a brisk,

invigorating chant suitable for raising power in a spell
or ritual for this purpose.

Exercise #9: Chanting by the Seat of Your Pants

Go outside somewhere you won't be disturbed—
preferably an inspiring place, such as a park or a
beach. Walk around until something in your surround-
ings suggests a topic to you. Then talk about it, out
loud, playing with different sounds and phrases until
you develop a chant that you like.

Exercise #10: Chant Repair

Here is a rough draft of a circle-casting chant. It
has some good concepts, but the phrasing is still loose.
Tighten it up to make it more punchy.

Cast a magic circle
Holding hands so fast and firm
Wrap its warmth
Around us

Exercise #11: Learning by Teaching

Go back and look at the chants you wrote for
Exercises 1, 5, or 6. Choose the one that seems easi-
est to learn. Then teach your chant to someone else.
How long did it take for your student to learn the chant?
Did you get any positive feedback or constructive criti-
cism? Write about your experiences in your journal.

Exercise #12: Compare and Contrast

Review the chants you composed for Exercises 7,
8, or 9. Compare and contrast them. Which method
of composition did you find easiest to use? Hardest?
Which chant is the most powerful? What similarities
and differences can you find among the chants? Journal your findings.

Chapter Eight: Preparing Powerful Prayers

In all human cultures, we find spirituality and religion in myriad guises. Along with them come prayers in a multitude of forms. Some inner sense attunes us to the Divine and alerts us to the presence of holiness. Furthermore, it urges us to reach out and connect with that numinous force, in whatever manner we may know it.

That urge to converse with God/dess—to *pray*—becomes stronger the more keen our need, the more desperate our situation. Devout people may pray daily, though others may pray only occasionally. In dire straits, even those who previously disbelieved in Divinity may find a prayer bubbling up from deep within them, driven forth by the pressure of the moment and the frantic search for someone, anyone, to aid them.

Happily, most of our prayers emerge in more ordinary circumstances. With religion comes liturgy, and the prayers for everyday use or for special occasions. You may wish to learn these, and some of the performance-based exercises in other chapters will help you deliver prayers in a more compelling fashion. But prayers, similar to spells, address a personal need or desire, so to focus precisely on your own concerns, you will need to compose your own prayers.

Addressing the Divine

A prayer is, first and foremost, communication with a god, goddess, or other higher power. In some religions, followers pray only to the top deity; in other religions, prayers may be addressed to a wide range of subordinate deities, saints, angels, devas, and other beneficent spirits. Certain traditions pray instead to ancestral or animal spirits. For simplicity's sake, I use "deity" to mean the entity to whom the prayer is addressed, but there are other options.

People customarily pray to deities with whom they have a close and ongoing relationship. Thus, choosing a deity to pray to is usually simple. Blessings may be sought from less-familiar deities, widening the field of choice. The discussion of choosing an appropriate deity appears in the following chapter. Those of you who pray to a lot of different patrons may wish to read that section in light of our current discussion on addressing deities.

Think of a prayer as a special kind of conversation with someone you revere. When you address the Divine, you should chiefly follow the customs of your tradition; or if you are a solitary, the preferences of your patron deity as best you understand them. Secondarily, take into account your own tastes and those of any other mortal witnesses to the prayer. Always compose and deliver prayers with awe and reverence.

Many Pagans worship deities from foreign cultures, which means that patron and follower may speak different native languages. Some Pagan prayers survive from ancient times in a great many tongues, and others include only a word or a line in a foreign language. Never put anything in a prayer just because it sounds good if you don't know what it means! However, *learning* a sacred language—even just a little bit—shows your sincerity. It connects you to the ancestors who spoke it and worshipped in it. Deities who rarely hear their native tongue spoken in prayer anymore are delighted when they do, which may incline them favorably toward followers who make the effort.

In your prayer, you need to inform your divine patron of various things. First, that the topic of your prayer falls within the deity's *sphere of influence*, the portion of the world for which a power is responsible, such as oceans for Neptune or marriage for Freya. The correct title or *epithet* establishes this beyond dispute: Neptune, Lord of the Deeps; or Vanabruð (which means "Bride of the Vanir," one of Freya's titles).[1] Second, that it is worthwhile to listen to your prayer. Most deities enjoy attention; simply calling their names and adding appropriate greetings or praises will suffice. Others hate to be bothered, and expect sacrifices or lavish promises. Third, if you make a request, you must go further, convincing the deity that your request is reasonable and lies within the deity's power to grant. Asking for outlandish boons lowers your chance of success. Asking for things a deity has granted you before, or routinely grants to petitioners, raises your chance of success—and it's perfectly acceptable to mention examples: "Hear me, Kuan Yin, you who hear the weeping of the world; comfort me, as you comfort all those who have yet to attain enlightenment."

Ask politely for what you need, and you may offer sacrifices or services in return for requests granted. Some prayers, in essence, take the form of a contract in which you present terms for an exchange between yourself and your patron.[2] You absolutely *must keep* any promise to a deity that you make in a prayer!

It is important to foster a bond between patron and follower. In writing prayers, you may seek to demonstrate your piety by listing things you have done or will do that further that deity's interests. Lavish praise is another popular bonding technique, which works well in some traditions, but not so well in others. Devotional prayers, performed regularly, also strengthen the bond.

Consider posture both in composing and delivering prayers. Body stance and hand signs help direct prayers to specific deities, some of whom have prescribed postures. Shape a triangle with your hands when addressing the Goddess; sign the horns when addressing the Horned God. These things can also indicate the prayer's theme. Kneel for prayers of humility and supplication; stand for prayers of power and celebration. Bow your head in respect to the dead. Remove your shoes when standing on holy ground. Different religions have particular rules for postures and actions that accompany prayers, so do your homework.

Prayer both reminds us of our needs and gives us a way to meet them. It invites the higher powers to intervene in our lives, when otherwise they might refrain out of respect for our free will (or preoccupation with other duties). People may pray for their own benefit, or for the benefit of others. In all cases, prayer forms a vital link between divinity and humanity. Whenever you address the Divine, you strengthen that link.

Parts of a Prayer

When composing prayers, it helps to break them down into their component parts. A prayer resembles a letter: It has an address, a greeting, a main body, and a closing. Imagine a pantheon as a large company that provides necessary goods and services. The gods, goddesses, and other figures are the people who make up the company. The pantheon's followers are customers, who sometimes need to communicate with the company. So people pray, which is similar to sending a letter; and a well-written prayer will reach the right deity and achieve your desired result.

Address

The name(s) and title(s) of your intended patron(s) determine where the prayer goes, just as the address on a letter does. You may address your prayer to just one deity, or several who share a common interest, the way you would send a letter to someone you already know. Some religions encourage people to pray directly to the supreme power in that pantheon, as would a company whose top executive is still involved in product development. Other religions encourage people to pray to powers in charge of specific themes, on the premise that the supreme power is busy with such things as lighting stars, and not well suited for solving problems on a human scale—as would a company whose top executive is focused on broad economic trends. Address your prayer accordingly.

It is vital to use the correct name (and pronunciation, when reading the prayer aloud) for a deity, to insure clear reception of the prayer. Sometimes, a sphere of influence may be so old that the name of the deity responsible for it has been forgotten; other times, a topic may be so new that it does not yet have a patron widely known for overseeing it. In such cases, it is appropriate to address the prayer based on descriptive qualities rather than individual names or characteristics—rather like addressing a letter to a job title (head publicist) or a department (publicity department) at a large company. You may wish to avoid using gendered pronouns, if you don't know whether the intended deity is masculine, feminine, or otherwise; or you may include a phrase such as "whether you be god or goddess."[3]

A related point concerns the naming of people, places, or things to benefit from the prayer. Sometimes you'll have an individual beneficiary in mind, but other times you'll want your prayer to cover a broad category of beneficiaries. Thus, it is acceptable to set beneficiaries by description rather than by name. Many famous prayers do this. Some common examples of descriptive beneficiaries include "the poor," "those who hunger," and "ancestors whose names have been forgotten."

Greeting

Prayers typically include a few phrases or lines that take the form of hails or praises speaking directly to the deity. They are similar to the greeting in a letter, in which you get the person's attention and exchange pleasantries before getting down to business. (To a certain extent, this may overlap the address.) Some deities have customary hails, which you can find in traditional sources and use in your own prayers. Other deities do not have specific hails, and you'll need to compose your own. For those, you may draw inspiration from traditional hails for other deities, or start from scratch.

Body

The main part of a prayer, similar to the body of a letter, can contain just about anything. Certain traditions set their own expectations here, such as mythic references. Asatru prayers customarily boast of heroic deeds by the gods, Druidic prayers relate one's place in Nature, Christian prayers acknowledge Christ's sacrifice, Buddhist prayers describe the path to enlightenment, and so forth.

This is also where the "give and take" exchanges in a prayer appear. You may list things you have done (or refrained from doing) in accordance with your patron's guidelines: "I have walked softly upon the sacred Earth"; promise goods or services to the gods in exchange for what you have received or hope to receive from them: "I will plant an oak tree in the yard of my new home, to honor the Earth spirits who helped me find a place to live"; ask for what you need: "May I always enjoy prosperity and security in my new home," or, "Let it be that storms pass by my house in peace, shedding only welcome rain"; express appreciation for your patron's help: "Thank you for guiding me to a comfortable house that I could afford." Phrases such as "I have," "I will," "May I," "Let it," and "Thank you" make good opening phrases for a set of parallel lines, a common feature in prayers.

Closing

A prayer needs a clear conclusion—a word or phrase that brings things to an end. In group prayers, this is usually spoken in chorus. Christian prayers famously end with "Amen." Afro-Caribbean prayers may end with "Ashé," and Wiccan prayers often end with "So mote it be" or "Blessed be." This way everyone knows when the prayer is finished.

Silence

After you finish praying, you should wait for a time in silence. This quiet time works similarly to the return address on a letter. It gives you a chance to reflect on what you've said and to receive a response. It's hardly fair to holler at the gods and then run off without waiting for an answer! Silence encourages reverence for the Divine and tranquility within the follower; it improves communication between the two, and makes prayer more effective.

Types of Prayers

Prayers come in many forms and functions, with features appropriate to each. Here we'll look at some of the major types of prayers and their characteristics.

First, prayers may consist of poetry or prose. Certain poetic forms, such as list poems, work especially well as prayers. The Bible, a famous source of prayers, is written in verses. Prose prayers tend to use their own techniques, such as repetition and alliteration. Long prose prayers can resemble myths, as they list the exploits of the gods, or they can resemble contracts, as they lay out the detailed exchange of promises between human and divine participants.

Prayers may be private or public. Private prayers usually involve a one-on-one communication between a follower and a patron deity. The details then depend on the personal tastes of those two participants. Public prayers may be performed by a whole group, and in this case they should be short and simple, with words that remain clear when spoken by many people together.

Alternatively, public prayers may be performed as a *litany*, with one person reading out a majority of the text and the audience giving a shorter, unified response. These prayers may have more elaborate text in the main part, and they must include clear cues for the audience to respond: For instance, a coven might always use "In the Lady's name" to cue everyone to chorus "So mote it be!" Public prayers work closer to a petition than a letter: Everybody adds their audible "signature" to the same document. It is essential for the audience to respond vigorously and harmoniously, in order for the deity to perceive the prayer as collective rather than individual. The most effective group prayers share a certain incantational quality: The audience need not follow along in a text, just repeat a simple and consistent response. This makes the prayers more accessible to people who have a hard time reading.

Prayers may be *obligatory, traditional,* or *spontaneous.* Obligatory prayers have a set form; followers of that religion must say those exact words at the prescribed times. These figure into mainstream religions far more than Pagan religions. Traditional prayers cover those issues that a deity expects to arise frequently, so they have a standard form that yields a standard response—as does exchanging form letters for routine services. Spontaneous prayers deal with unusual situations that do not neatly fit anything available on the list of traditional prayers. These are similar to personal letters, in which you describe what's going on and what you'd like to have happen next.

Most prayers you compose will be spontaneous. However, you may fall in love with one, and decide to repeat it on every full moon; or a group of people may decide to draft an *ordinary* to be performed on all occasions of a certain type. These then become part of a tradition. For instance, a coven that specializes in healing circles might create a prayer to be said by anyone in the community who needs healing, as a means of accessing the power raised in ritual.

Some common types of prayers, based on structure and purpose, include the following:

Bid Prayers

In this type of prayer, the High Priestess or High Priest leads an audience in silent prayer. The name comes from some classic prayers that use phrases such as "I bid you to pray for..." as a means of directing attention to a particular concern, although contemporary ones may say "Let us pray...." This technique works well in medium-sized groups, and excels in huge groups where constant collective speech would be overwhelming. It's also the preferred form for certain types of memorial, because it includes a "moment of silence" for everyone to insert their own prayers; and for civic or interfaith prayers, when people need to pray without imposing the details on human bystanders.

First, the leader names the cause and bids people to pray. Then comes a space for the audience to pray silently. Next, the leader summarizes those prayers in a collective fashion. (Leaders may bid prayers for just one cause, or for several in succession.) Finally, the leader concludes the prayer, calling on everyone to make a single response out loud, such as "Blessed be!"

Bid prayers are formulaic and easy to write. Your opening should tell the audience what you'll be doing and what they should do. If you're addressing a single deity, include a hail to that deity; if you're leaving the audience free to address deities of their choice, instead make a general address such as "to whom it may concern" or, "Hear our prayers, divine powers." Make each bid brief and specific; if you do more than one, keep them parallel in phrasing. Wait a consistent amount of time for silent prayers. (Practice even pacing without glancing at your watch; it takes a while to develop this skill.) Allow 10 to 15 seconds for a prayer consisting of several bids; for a single solemn bid, as in a memorial, allow one full minute. The summary can run somewhat longer than the bid; use it to say the kinds of things you hope people are saying silently.

Conclude the prayer with an appreciation of divine attention, and cue the audience to give their collective response.

Here is a bid prayer for a Pagan festival in which people want to focus on environmental issues:

"Gaia Bid" by Elizabeth Barrette

High Priestess: "I bid you to pray for the purity of Air."
[silence for prayer]
High Priest: "Gaia, you have blessed us with clean air to breathe. Clear our minds that we may think of solutions to the problems we face. Lend us your aid as we struggle to protect the air from smog and greenhouse gasses. Blessed be!"
All: "Blessed be!"

High Priestess: "I bid you to pray for the sanctity of Fire."
[silence for prayer]
High Priest: "Gaia, you have blessed us with fire to burn away the old. Ignite our souls as we fight for the environment. Help us understand that certain ecosystems need fires, and teach us how to manage them safely. Blessed be!"
All: "Blessed be!"

High Priestess: "I bid you to pray for the clarity of Water."
[silence for prayer]
High Priest: "Gaia, you have blessed us with clear water to drink. Refresh our hearts as we restore what has been polluted. Guide our efforts to heal the rivers and oceans of the world. Blessed be!"
All: "Blessed be!"

High Priestess: "I bid you pray for the security of Earth."
[silence for prayer]

> High Priest: "Gaia, you have blessed us with rich land to live on. Nourish our bodies as we steward our homes. Show us how to build, and grow, and live in a sustainable manner. Blessed be!"
> All: "Blessed be!"

Cyclic Prayers

Most prayers are meant to be performed once. Cyclic prayers, however, are designed to be repeated for a specific number of days (or nights). They typically request a special favor from the Divine, such as healing, and are usually performed in private. One example is the *Novena*, practiced by Catholics, in which a prayer is recited once a day for nine days—either the same lines, or one section per day.[4] An *octave* is an eight-day prayer. Afro-Caribbean traditions favor seven-day cycles.

You can find candles specially made to accompany nine-day or seven-day prayers. Glass candles come in various sizes and colors, often several colors within a single glass. Free-standing knob candles usually have seven knobs, one for each day in the cycle.

The most important part of a cyclic prayer is the number of repetitions, which can be any number greater than one. Choose a number sacred to your patron deity, or magically relevant to your topic: 2 (love, balance), 3 (creativity, control, activity), 4 (structure, rest, health), 5 (conflict, communication), 6 (friendship, money), 7 (magic, spirituality, change, travel), 8 (strength, stability, secrets), 9 (courage, completion, holiness).[5] You will repeat the prayer this number of times. You may also wish to subdivide the prayer into this many verses or paragraphs.

Repetition provides the main power source for cyclic prayers. Take advantage of this by repeating names, titles, opening phrases, or entire lines. Cyclic prayers should be performed at the same time each day; for instance, at dawn, at 3 p.m., or at bedtime. Stating the time within the prayer text adds emphasis and energy. In other respects the composition is similar to other prayer types.

This seven-day prayer pleads for a solution to a problem that seems insoluble, and would work well with a white seven-knob candle.

"Looking Everywhere for an Answer"
by Elizabeth Barrette

I pray seven times for an answer:

First day if it comes from the east

Second day if it comes from the south

Third day if it comes from the west

Fourth day if it comes from the north

Fifth day if it comes from below

Sixth day if it comes from above

Seventh day if it comes from within.

I pray seven times so that I may receive the answer

To my problem, no matter where it comes from.

Daily Devotions

Spiritual awareness deepens when you set aside a little time each day for prayer, most often in the morning or evening. You may say the same prayer every day (for example, a salute to the sun or the moon), rotate through a specific set (one for each day of the week), or use a new one every time to suggest a theme for the day (such as found in books or calendars offering a year's worth of devotions). In solitary use, they strengthen the bond between deity and follower. In group use, they aid unity—a nice touch for the morning or evening circle at a festival.

Devotions work best when they get right to the point, so keep them simple. A common format begins with a quote from a myth or other sacred source, followed by a comment on the message or lesson it contains: inspiration and reflection.

To compose such a devotion, choose an inspiring quote from your tradition's mythic resources, then write in your own words what that passage means. Devotions are an ideal place to explore the ways in which ancient lore applies to modern life.

Another type of devotion offers advice on living, a kind of touchstone as you go through your day. Consider this Taoist comparison of various goals:

> He who knows other men is discerning; he who knows himself is intelligent. He who overcomes others is strong; he who overcomes himself is mighty. He who is satisfied with his lot is rich; he who goes on acting with energy has a (firm) will. He who does not fail in the requirements of his position, continues long; he who dies and yet does not perish, has longevity.[6]

Offertory Prayers

Sometimes the reason for inviting the Divine to listen is that you're giving something away. This may be a direct offering, such as fancy incense burned on the altar; or it may be indirect, such as collecting food for a charity, in honor of the gods. The context may be private, as when fulfilling a promise to your patron; or public, as when taking donations from a large group. Offertory prayers provide balance for those times when we request things through prayer—because no one, not even a deity, enjoys hearing nothing but "gimme gimme gimme!" all the time.

When composing offertory prayers, consider themes of giving, receiving, generosity, humility, energy exchange, and abundance. Preferably, name the offering itself; describing it in detail adds to the impact of the prayer. It is also prudent to state who is giving and receiving the offering. Avoid asking for anything, unless it directly relates to the offering ("Fill us with generosity"). Well-written offertory prayers enhance the joy of giving, please the gods, and encourage people to be more generous.

This Hindu prayer addresses Agni, the god of fire, whose sacrificial flame is tended by a special priest.

"Hymn to Agni" by Marah Ellis Ryan

I implore Agni, the chief priest, the divine minister of the sacrifice, the Hotri priest, the best giver of wealth.

Agni, worthy to be implored by former poets and by new, may he bring the gods hither!

Through Agni man gained wealth, satisfying even day by day, glorious wealth of vigorous kindred.

Agni, the offering which thou encirclest on all sides, that alone goes to the gods.

Agni, the Hotri priest, the wise counsellor, the truthful, the most glorious, may he, the God, come with the gods!

Whatever wealth thou, Agni, shalt bestow on the sacrificer, thine it will be, forsooth, Agni.

To thee, O Agni, we come day by day, bringing praise in mind, O Illuminator of Darkness!

To thee, the Lord of sacrifices, the bright Guarder of the Law, who art growing in thy own house.

Thou then, O Agni, be gracious to us like as a father to his son; stay with us for our welfare!

Petition and Intercession

These prayers make requests. Prayers of *petition* ask something for yourself, prayers of *intercession* ask something for another person or cause, and the two may overlap when a prayer details several related requests. People request all manner of things—healing, prosperity, easy childbirth, spiritual enlightenment, magical ability, a new home, peace of mind—anything they need from within a patron deity's sphere of influence.

The trick here lies in making the request specific enough to achieve the desired result, but not so specific that it hampers divine creativity. State what you need (and remember to ask, rather than demanding), then allow that the universe may think of a better solution than yours. Intercessory prayers also need to allow room for the other person's Will to participate. When making requests, you may also promise something in return and offer thanks for your patron's aid.

The following example, as do many Native American prayers, combines petition and intercession.

"The White House Prayer"
by Washington Matthews

In Kininaékai.

In the house made of dawn.

In the story made of dawn.

On the trail of dawn.

O, Talking God!

His feet, my feet, restore (or heal).

His limbs, my limbs, restore.

His body, my body, restore.

His mind, my mind, restore.

His voice, my voice, restore.

His plumes, my plumes, restore.

With beauty before him, with beauty before me.

With beauty behind him, with beauty behind me.

With beauty above him, with beauty above me.

With beauty below him, with beauty below me.

With beauty around him, with beauty around me.

With pollen beautiful in his voice, with pollen beautiful in my voice.

It is finished in beauty.

It is finished in beauty.

Praises

Prayers of praise salute higher powers or their works. These play a vital role in celebrating holy days dedicated to a specific deity. They can create or strengthen the bond between a patron deity and a follower. Yet praises also well up spontaneously when we encounter something awe-inspiring such as a sunset, an ocean, or a newborn infant. In those moments, we perceive the world as Art, which brings to mind its Artist; and we take the role of audience, expressing our admiration. Some traditions teach that our appreciation helps shape the world, by empowering the things we praise and diminishing those we ignore.

To compose a praise prayer, first study your subject intensely. Absorb every detail. If you are writing about deities, read their myths, study their sacred sites, explore their sphere of influence. If you are writing about an object, investigate it with all your senses. Focus on the emotions that your subject evokes in you. Now put the two together, expressed outward, through words.

Write ardently. You may sweep past your subject in a surge of excitement, shedding brief, vivid phrases. You may caress your subject slowly with a description that lingers over each feature in turn. Imagine what it was before, and what it could become; speak to its existence in the flow of time, as a sturdy or ephemeral thing. Seek concrete nouns and active verbs, then adorn them with voluptuous modifiers. Use your dictionary and thesaurus to find glorious words to describe your subject—preferably uncommon words that create a fresh perspective. Don't get stuck on ordinary terms such as "great" or "beautiful." Go for words such as "illustrious" or "resplendent."

The core message of a praise prayer is "I love you" or "I love what you have made." It exists chiefly to admire, a selfless and fulfilling act. Here is a prayer in praise of the Roman goddess Diana:

"To Diana" by Charles G. Leland

Lovely Goddess of the bow!
Lovely Goddess of the arrows!
Of all hounds and of all hunting
Thou who wakest in starry heaven
When the sun is sunk in slumber
Thou with moon upon thy forehead,
Who the chase by night preferrest
Unto hunting in the daylight,
With thy nymphs unto the music
Of the horn—thyself the huntress,
And most powerful: I pray thee
Think, although but for an instant,
Upon us who pray unto thee!

Thanksgiving Prayers

These prayers, also called *gratitudes,* are thank-you notes to the Divine. Similar to offertory prayers, they veer away from the "gimme" approach that most prayers take. Expressing thanks honors the gods for their efforts to make life easier, uplifts the spirit by cultivating a grateful attitude, and improves the chance of the gods doing more favors for an appreciative audience. This also helps you focus on what you have, rather than on what you lack.

When writing prayers of thanksgiving, concentrate on your feelings of gratitude. Celebrate what you have received. You may list several things, or describe just one thing in depth. Give thanks for little things as well as big things. We are most moved to express gratitude for momentous occasions, such as reaching home safely through a terrible storm. Yet most of life consists of prosaic and whimsical tidbits, like the thousands of tiles that make up a mosaic, so give thanks for warm flannel sheets and pouncy kittens and whatever else makes you smile.

As with spells, keep your phrasing positive rather than negative: "I give thanks for prosperity" not "I am thankful that I don't have too many bills." Avoid asking for anything not directly related to appreciation; for example, "May I always remember to give thanks, and find more things to be grateful for." Always include words such as "thanks," "thank you," "gratitude," "appreciation," and so on in such prayers.

Here is a prayer of thanksgiving for the day's end:

"Gratitude at Twilight" by Elizabeth Barrette

Thank you for the passing of the light.

Thank you for the purple clouds that creep.

Thank you for the stars, the moon, the night.

Thank you for the gentle arms of sleep.

Composing Prayers

Prayers are among the easiest magical compositions to create. The structured ones tend to be formulaic, allowing you to identify a pattern and "fill in the blanks" based on your circumstances. The less structured ones can be quite free, allowing you to express yourself in your own words. The underlying approach is similar though. Some specific points of composition have already appeared in the previous discussion of prayer types; now let's look at prayer composition in general.

To compose a prayer, decide on the topic and create an opening to get your patron's attention. Use your own experiences to form the main body of your prayer. Describe your relationship to your divine patron. Talk about how your words, deeds, and beliefs further the deity's goals. Explain what you need and why. Express thanks for benefits received. Then close.

Keep it simple. Choose one unifying theme or metaphor per prayer. If you try to do too much at once, you'll obscure the message. Make sure that everything relates to your purpose. Likewise, say what you need to say and then stop. A short, passionate prayer works better than a long, rambling one.

Pay attention to the structure of your prayer. If it includes parallels, as many prayers do, keep the phrases equivalent. A common mistake involves mixing different kinds of subjects within the same set, for example:

We pray for:

o All who live in fear of war, or dread acts of terrorism.

o Those who fear they must prepare for. violence, not knowing where it may strike next.

o People whose job it is to teach others to fear.[7]

See how the first two pray for victims, and the third prays for perpetrators? Avoid mixing positive and negative—things you want and things you don't want, people whom you want to help and people whom you want to hinder, and so on. If you pray for mixed subjects in the same fashion, especially within the same prayer, then you may get the same *result* applied to everything in the set. That would be bad.

Collect things that make good prayer components: words frequently used in your tradition, deity names and titles, kennings, phrases used to activate specific parts of a prayer, and so on. Use key phrases and repetition to help yourself (and your audience, in public) keep the place in a prayer. Use kennings to create a sense of mystery, raise power, and evoke a specific tradition. Dip into this treasure trove of ideas when you aren't sure what to say next.

You should use terms that feel comfortable to you. Avoid overly ornate words and sentences if they make you feel silly instead of reverent. Also avoid picking up baggage from other traditions' prayers. Look for examples and inspiration, then write from your heart and make your prayers original.

Bear in mind the focus of your prayer. The main goal is to communicate with your patron deity, so that's who you should address. Some prayers are partly intended for a human audience, and those intended for public use should be designed accordingly. But it's generally not a good idea to "speak sideways," saying things in a prayer (ostensibly aimed at a deity) that are really meant for the bystanders. Keep the lines of address clear.

If you get stuck while composing a prayer, there are several options for getting unstuck. First, make variations on a theme through repetition and parallels. Suppose you've already got a good line that begins "Let it be...." Copy the phrase "Let it be that..." several more times, creating a set of repetitions with a meaningful number. Look at the end of the good line and analyze its structure: For instance, it might have a concrete noun followed by an action with a positive outcome. Using that pattern, lay out more nouns and good things that could happen to them, and thereby fill in the rest of those lines.

Names and titles of deities make excellent filler. If you need something to fill a gap based on a specific rhyme, stress pattern, number of syllables, alliterative sound, or other feature, then check your "cast list." You can also use the common-word list for your tradition. Most prayers put this type of content towards the beginning; however, some also put it at the end. A few scatter it throughout, as part of the structure, particularly call-and-response prayers intended to be performed by large groups.

Finally, some deities will let you essentially filibuster, if you can't think of what to say next! Mythic references often make a good starting place; for instance, Thor rarely gets tired of hearing a priestess brag about his battles. Conversely, Native American traditions emphasize humility; there, you can riff endlessly on, "I am small, I am weak, I am insignificant in the vastness of the world." Each tradition has its own favorite areas on which to expound. Learn the ones for your tradition; they're especially useful if you need to make up prayers on the spot for an urgent occasion.

Of all magical compositions, prayers are among the most likely to become necessary on short notice, as well as those planned in advance. They serve many different purposes both in public and in private spiritual observances. So it's a good idea to practice composing prayers at leisure, and in different forms for different purposes, so that you'll be able to produce what's needed if you ever find yourself in a situation that urgently needs a prayer.

Exercises

Use the following exercises to practice writing prayers. You may do them all in order, or pick and choose. You may want to switch back and forth between this and Chapter Nine, as both deal with spiritual compositions. Because prayers can be prose or poetry, consider doing some of these exercises twice, once for each.

Exercise #1: Conversations With the Gods

What deity do you pray to most often? What is your patron deity in charge of? What do their myths sound like? What other things are associated with your patron? Use these to shape your communication. Imagine a conversation between you and your patron, and write down both halves.

Exercise #2: Prayers as Messages

Explore the idea of prayer as a "letter" to your patron deity. Write a prayer in the form of a letter, including each of the parts described in this chapter.

Exercise #3: Private Prayer

Choose a type of prayer that works well in a solitary setting, such as a daily devotion, thanksgiving, or cyclic prayer. Write a prayer of that type on the topic of prosperity.

Exercise #4: Public Prayer

Imagine yourself at a summer festival where people of various Earth-based belief systems have gathered to celebrate the season. Discussion around the evening fire reveals that many people would like to try public prayer in a Pagan context. Think over some types of prayer that work well in groups—praises, bid prayers, offertory prayers, petition and intercession—then compose a prayer for this occasion.

Exercise #5: Metaphorically Speaking

Many famous prayers contain metaphors. It's not always easy to frame ephemeral concepts in concrete language. Figurative speech helps by comparing the ephemeral to something more familiar. Write a prayer using an extended metaphor to illuminate a complex theological topic, comparing the individual parts of each.

Exercise #6: Give and Take

Reread "Hymn to Agni." Although it is explicitly an offertory prayer, as indicated by such phrases as "the offering which thou encirclest on all sides," it also includes some requests, such as "bring the gods hither," and "stay with us for our welfare." Rewrite this composition to remove all the "gimme" language and redirect the emphasis to the offering.

Exercise #7: Make Me One With Everything

The following Peruvian prayer combines praise and petition, addressing the ineffable and unknowable spirit in charge of all creation. Using this as an example, compose a prayer to a deity whose name you don't know, or a power you consider to be unknowable.

"Hymn to the Unknown God" by Marah Ellis Ryan

O RULER! Lord of the universe,
Whether thou art male,
Whether thou art female,
Lord of reproduction
Wherever thou mayest be!
O Lord of divination
Where art thou?
Thou mayest be above,
Thou mayest be below,
Or perhaps around
Thy splendid throne and sceptre.
O hear me!
From the sky above,
In which thou mayest be,
From the sea beneath
In which thou mayest be.
Creator of the world,
Maker of all men;
Lord of all Lords
My eyes fail me for longing to see thee
For the sole desire to know thee.
O look down upon me
For thou knowest me.
The sun—the moon—
The day—the night—
Spring—winter,
Are not ordained in vain
By thee, O Deity!
They all travel
To the assigned place;

They all arrive
At their destined ends
Whithersoever thou pleasest.
Thy royal scepter
Thou holdest.
O hear me!
O choose me!
Let it not be
That I should tire,
That I should die!

Chapter Nine:
Bestowing Beautiful
Blessings

A blessing is a unique magical composition in that it serves to channel divine power through the speaker. A priest or priestess may do this directly, as when issuing blessings as a holy person: "By the power vested in me, I bless this marriage." One may also do it indirectly, as when calling on a deity to provide a blessing: "Demeter, we ask you to bless this garden."

Blessings serve multiple purposes. They can indicate formal approval and support: "You have my blessing to form a new coven." They can bestow divine protection, favor, or other benefits: "In the name of Thor, may a mighty shield be upon you." They can consecrate a person, place, or thing: "Powers of Air, bless this athame as a tool of Art." The deities, phrasing, and goals may vary, but the basic process remains similar.

Choosing Appropriate Deities

First, consider the similarities and differences between prayers and blessings. Prayers chiefly send energy from the human to the Divine; blessings are a way of receiving energy from the Divine. Prayers typically address a deity with whom the speaker already has a relationship. Blessings, however, might be needed for all sorts of things that fall under the responsibility of many different deities. Thus, an important part of composing a blessing lies in choosing a relevant deity.

One method is to start with a broad field and narrow it down. Take a pantheon and look within it for the deity whose sphere of influence matches the topic of your intended blessing. If you follow a specific path already, look in that pantheon or its near neighbors. For instance, Hellenic Pagans should use the Greek pantheon, and look next to the Roman pantheon if the Greek does not suffice. Even if you ask a blessing from deities other than your personal patron(s), they will have some familiarity due to sharing the same or related tradition.

If you don't belong to a specific tradition, you can still use this technique. Simply trace what tradition(s) your ancestors would have followed, or the tradition(s) historically indigenous to the place you live. Thus, a Japanese-American would explore pantheons from Japan. A land-blessing in North America would involve looking into the local tribal religion. *The Gods of Man: A Small Dictionary of Pagan Gods and Goddesses* by David W. Owens offers a brief look at deities sorted by geographic region or culture.

Another method involves searching for the specific intersection point between deity and topic. Many books and online resources feature lists of deities and their spheres of influence. Some expand on this to give a kind of biography for each deity; others just give the name and a set of themes. D.J. Conway's *Lord of Light and Shadow: The Many Faces of the God* and Patricia Monaghan's *The New Book of Goddesses & Heroines* contain indexes of deity names and attributes. Online, use your favorite search engine to find intersections by typing in combinations such as "love goddess" or "sky god."

Your search for suitable deities may turn up just one name, or several. At this stage, check to make sure that you can meet each deity's expectations. Some are worshipped only by people of a certain sex or life status, or only at specific times or places. Others expect particular activities, offerings, abstentions, or other rites. Some are open-minded and straightforward to work with; others are picky and easily offended. Remember that asking for a blessing is asking for a favor, so choose a deity whom you can reasonably persuade to grant it.

Channeling Divine Energy

There are two broad types of blessings as distinguished by their energy. Direct blessings come from a holy person who holds a pool of divine energy within him- or herself. This resource, regularly replenished by a patron deity, is part of what enables a priest or priestess to do his or her spiritual work. It functions as a wellspring from which water may be drawn at need. Indirect blessings can come through anyone, using the spirit as a conduit for divine energy. This works similarly to turning on a faucet and running water through a hose. Although the handling is a little different for the person delivering the blessing, the ultimate source remains the same— it's all divine energy.

As I mentioned, holy people have a certain reservoir of power. Part of the consecration of a priest or priestess involves creating this reservoir, and making a connection with some divine source(s) to keep it filled. Different traditions have their own ways and times for accomplishing this. In some it happens as part of first-degree or later initiation. In others, it involves a whole separate investiture ceremony.

If you have been through such a process, then this pool of divine energy is what you'll be dipping into when you bestow direct blessings. Reach within yourself to find that divine energy, which is inside you, but not of you. Call it up, and pour forth a portion of it to the person who has asked for your blessing. Remember also to take time in your devotions for replenishing your wellspring of energy.

Certain occasions incline people to ask the blessing of a spiritual mentor. Handfasting, baby naming, initiation, and the beginning of a quest are common examples. Your tradition may provide you with words or phrases to use on these occasions, or you may receive divine inspiration on the spot. Take such requests seriously, and deliver the best blessing you can in words and energy, for these are significant moments.

Everyone has the capacity to channel divine energy. Some people find it easier than others, and practice improves the skill considerably. The challenge is that most activities require you to "do" something, such as the way spellcraft relies on using your Will to influence reality. Conversely, channeling requires you to "be" something—a conduit—and that means you have to get your Will out of the way. The harder you try, the less it will work, as if you were squeezing a water hose and choking off the flow. In this regard, the functions required for magical and spiritual work are direct opposites.

The key to effective channeling is to cultivate a relaxed and receptive state of awareness. Think of holding a water hose in your hands, firmly enough to control its direction, but gently enough to let the water flow freely. Concentrate on the higher power whose energy you wish to channel. When you deliver a blessing, the divine energy should flow through you to the subject of the blessing and create the desired effect.

People channel things all the time; different types of energy in different ways. Each person's creative abilities invite certain expressions to manifest. A sculptor allows three-dimensional art to emerge in clay, metal, or wood; a musician shapes sound through instruments; an energy worker draws on the healing forces to promote health. A writer channels ideas into words—and writers rely heavily on inspiration to guide them.

When you set out to compose a blessing, open yourself to the Divine; you may find yourself channeling words as well as energy. Sometimes when you are asked for a blessing, the right phrases will simply emerge. This is a perfectly admirable way of composing a blessing, and it is no less work than assembling one word-by-word. It's just a different type of work, requiring you to learn how to free your inner self of obstructions so that you make an ideal conduit for both words and energy. Regular prayer and meditation lay a good foundation for this; writing practice also helps.

In the absence of inspiration providing you with a ready-made blessing, you can assemble your own from scratch. The steps following, and the exercises at the end of the chapter, will walk you through this process.

Listing Benedictions

The first step in composing a blessing is to open yourself to divine energy and become receptive to input from the higher power of your choice. Take a few minutes to concentrate on your purpose. Write down any words or phrases that come to you; even fragmentary inspiration is useful and can be expanded into a complete blessing.

"Benediction" means "good words," and that's the core of a blessing. You may find it helpful to compile a list of terms commonly used in blessings. Open your favorite hardcopy or online thesaurus, such as *Roget's Thesaurus of English Words and Phrases* or Roget's Thesaurus Online. Use it to look up synonyms for "bless," "good," "health," "happy," "safe," "sacred," and so forth, which apply to many topics. Add words relating to your chosen deity's sphere of influence and ones used in the tradition's liturgy.

Speak in a style that your divine patron will appreciate. Logical arguments are likely to please the intellectual Athena, but the sensual Parvati would be more moved by emotional entreaties. Deities of inspiration such as Brigid or Apollo enjoy elaborate literary creations. Chango, the patron of iron and tools, might prefer that you get to the point with, "Help me find someone to teach me blacksmithing, and I will keep a shrine to you in my forge." Many traditional prayers are written in ornate, archaic language—you may use this if it appeals to you and your patron, but it's perfectly okay to speak plainly instead.

Decide what *voice* to use in your blessing. For a blessing from a holy person, use the first person: "As High Priestess of

Willownest Coven, I bless this infant born into our community...." When representing a deity in a ceremonial function,
also use the first person: "I, Selene, bless this pool to be a
mirror of the moon." To create an intimate mood, use the second person: "You go forth in peace and you return in peace,
with a blessing of safety upon you." For a narrative effect
(especially useful in blessing from a distance) use the third
person: "The blessing of Herne the Hunter softens his steps
and hides his scent as he enters the forest...."

As you can see in the previous examples, it is important
to specify who the blessing comes from. Use names, titles,
and voice to establish this. Also include who or what is to be
blessed. Kennings work well for these purposes. Consider this
Finnish blessing, which draws on the power of Ukko:

> **"Prayer of the Sower" by Marah Ellis Ryan**
> BLESSING to the seed I scatter,
> Where it falls upon the meadow,
> By the grace of Ukko mighty,
> Through the open finger spaces
> Of the hand that all things fashioned.
> Queen of meadow-land and pasture!
> Bid the earth unlock her treasures.
> Bid the soil the young seed nourish,
> Never shall their teeming forces
> Never shall their strength prolific
> Fail to nourish and sustain us
> If the Daughters of Creation,
> They, the free and bounteous givers
> Still extend their gracious favor
> Offer still their strong protection.
> Rise, O Earth! from out thy slumbers
> Bid the soil unlock her treasures!

Whether formed as prose or poetry, blessings often incorporate lists that describe complete coverage—for instance,
all the directions, all the parts of the body, or all the stages of

a journey. Choosing one of these gives you a framework to follow as you compose your blessing. (Be *thorough*. Mythology is full of stories about what happens when a blessing has a loophole in it.) Tables of correspondences can suggest more "sets" for you to use in this manner.

As in spells and some types of prayer, blessings need instruction. Describe what you want to happen and how. It is generally better to frame things in positive terms than in negative terms. However, some traditional blessings do take the negative form: "Nothing from the East may hinder him..." or, "So long as you bear this blessing, no blade shall pierce your flesh and no unkind word shall wound your spirit."

Employ the techniques you learned in Chapter Three for desired effects. To create a sense of flow and openness, use assonance. If your blessing rhymes, choose end-vowel rhymes. To create a sense of boundaries and barriers, use alliteration and end-consonant rhymes. To anchor your blessing firmly, use concrete nouns and strong active verbs. To connect the material world to the numinous, use symbolism. To give structure, consider parallels, a frequent element in blessings.

Finally, conclude your blessing with a line or phrase that wraps up the statement and sets things in motion. Conclusions used for spells (such as "So mote it be!") or prayers (such as "Ashé!") can apply to blessings as well.

Here is a prose blessing for a modern challenge:

"College Quest Blessing" by Elizabeth Barrette

Today you leave to make your way in the wider world; may your quest for education be blessed by all scholarly gods and goddesses. In the name of Odin, raven-bearing sage of the Norse, may your mind fly on the wind's wings. In the name of Brigid, Irish goddess of inspiration, may the flame of knowledge light your way. In the name of Thoth, great scribe of ancient Egypt, may your words endure for all time. In the name of Tara, star

goddess of India, may wisdom guide you every step
of the way. Be blessed in waking and sleeping; be
blessed in reading and writing; be blessed in
speaking and listening; be blessed in all ways and
all times. Blessed be!

Of all the composition types, blessings are the least about
you. They're about the Divine, and about the recipient(s). Remember that the more you can keep your Will out of the way,
the better the blessing will function—and likely, the easier a
time you will have composing it. Mastery of this composition
lies as much in spiritual practice as in writing practice, so
take care to balance the two.

Exercises

Use these exercises to practice composing blessings and channeling divine energy. You may pick and
choose, or do them all in order. You may want to alternate between this and Chapter Eight, as both deal
with spiritual compositions. Because blessings can
be prose or poetry, consider doing some of these exercises twice, once for each.

Exercise #1: Seeking Meaning

What does "blessing" mean to you? What kind(s)
of blessing(s) have you received in the past? What
kind(s) of blessing(s) do you most want to bestow?
Write down at least three occasions for which you
might decide to compose a blessing.

Exercise #2: Who's in Charge?

Look at your answers from Exercise #1, and choose
one of the blessing occasions. Do some research to
find two or more deities whose sphere of influence
includes that occasion. Who are they? Where do they
come from? How would you address them in a blessing?

Exercise #3: The Wellspring Within

Priests and priestesses benefit from practicing receptivity. Set aside some time to meditate, pray, or otherwise commune with the deity of your choice. Decide on something to bless, such as your home or a tree. Reach into your reservoir of divine energy and cup out a portion of it, as you would scoop water from a pool with your hands. Open your mind to inspiration and say whatever words of blessing come to you, as you release the energy with the words, like pouring water onto the earth.

Exercise #4: Opening the Way

Anyone can learn to channel divine energy consciously. Choose a blessing from a book or other resource. Concentrate on the deity who empowers the blessing. Imagine yourself at the doorway of your soul, opening the door and inviting the deity to pour energy through you. Take in as much divine energy as you comfortably can, letting it flow through you, and into the words as you read the blessing aloud. When you finish, imagine closing the door again.

Exercise #5: Comparative Brainstorming

Choose two topics for blessings, and one form. Sit down and write a blessing in your chosen form, using the first topic. Note how challenging you found it, whether inspiration flowed smoothly or you got stuck, and so forth. Wait one day. Then spend five minutes meditating or praying to clear your mind and open yourself to the Divine. Immediately upon completing this step, write a blessing in your chosen form, using the second topic. Was it easier or harder? Which blessing turned out better?

Exercise #6: Contemporary Quests

People often appreciate a blessing when embarking on an important journey or task. Reread "College

Quest Blessing." Using that as inspiration, compose a blessing for another occasion significant in modern life.

Exercise #6: Blessing Buildings

All manner of magical and spiritual compositions have been used to protect and sanctify the structures that people build. Here is a blessing in the original Gaelic and English translation:

"Beannachadh Taighe" by Alexander Carmichael

DHE, beannaich an taigh,
Bho steidh gu staidh,
Bho chrann gu fraigh,
Bho cheann gu saidh,
Bho dhronn gu traigh,
Bho sgonn gu sgaith,
Eadar bhonn agus bhraighe,
Bhonn agus bhraighe.

"Blessing of House"

GOD bless the house,
From site to stay,
From beam to wall,
From end to end,
From ridge to basement,
From balk to roof-tree,
From found to summit,
Found and summit.

Notice all the rhyme, assonance, and alliteration in the original Gaelic version. The English translation makes it easier to see the list effect as the house is covered in all its dimensions. Compose a blessing for a building or other manmade structure using a spatial organization similar to this.

Chapter Ten:
Writing Wonderful
Rituals—The Parts

Up to this point, we have explored individual types of composition. Some of those may appear in sets, such as matching
God and Goddess prayers. Others may include more than one
part, such as elaborate spells. However, most are singular
and can stand alone. Now we're going to explore a type of
composition that always takes a modular form.

A *ritual* is a detailed activity consisting of steps to perform
in a specific order; in the case of religious rituals, to achieve a
spiritual purpose. Thus, each ritual is actually a careful assembly of smaller compositions working together, much the
way a body consists of many organs and tissues animated by
a vital spirit. In this chapter, we'll look at some specialized
compositions that appear in rituals, and in the next chapter,
we'll discuss how to put them together to form an effective
ritual.

Writing plays many roles in ritual. Some rituals consist
entirely of poetry, others entirely of prose, but most contain a
mix of prose and poetry. Compositions may be spoken or sung,
and they should usually be performed in a loud, clear, commanding voice. The types of composition covered here in regard to ritual use are openings and closings, songs and stories,
invocations, evocations, and devocations. This chapter also
touches on some activities that may accompany the words,
as these often need to be written into the outline.

Openings and Closings

Every ritual has a beginning and an end. Both for safety and effectiveness, these require clear delineation. Openings and closings define the boundaries of a ritual in place and time, the way your skin encloses and protects the rest of your body. Always pair openings and closings! If you do one, make sure to do the other too, or it creates uncomfortable imbalances in energy.

Openings establish sacred, magical space. They help people shift from ordinary to heightened consciousness. They also focus attention and begin to stir energy. Casting a circle, as mentioned in Chapter Six, creates a protective barrier; most rituals therefore include it as part of the opening sequence.

Openings may address incorporeal entities or just the people in the circle. In this regard they also set the tone for the ritual: If the opening is elaborate and tightly structured, people expect a formal ceremony; if it is simple and free-flowing, it creates a more casual atmosphere. If you start off very structured and then turn spontaneous, or vice versa, you will disrupt the flow of magic, and—if working in a group—confuse your fellow practitioners. So make sure that your opening indicates what to expect from the ritual.

Closings return everything to reality after the work is done. They assist people in making the transition back to ordinary consciousness. They balance and release any residual energy in a safe and controlled manner. Similar to openings, they should match the tone of the ritual. Thus, closings may be a little simpler than openings because the main work is already done, but if they are too perfunctory then people may not have adequate time to readjust. Don't end the ritual with an abrupt drop back to the everyday world; let it down gently.

The opening is the first thing done in a ritual; the closing is the last thing done. They usually accompany some type of action on the part of the presenter. Openings and closings written for group rituals may include instructions for the attendees. Those for solitary rituals can be simpler.

Detailed openings and closings may be written in advance, then memorized or printed on cue cards for use in ritual. However, they are probably the most popular choice for spontaneous composition, especially at festivals where the leader may call for volunteers at the last minute. A good grasp of the purposes and principles allows you to compose openings and closings on the spot. Alternatively, communing with elemental and divine entities enhances your ability to channel the right words, much as we discussed in the previous chapter on blessings. Poetic openings and closings are often easier to memorize; prose ones are easier for most people to *ad lib*.

Openings and closings may be done in a variety of forms, rhymed or unrhymed, long or short. They should contain specific language describing their function. Some people count calling the Quarters (Air/East, Fire/South, Water/West, Earth/North) as an opening; others consider it an evocation. Both interpretations work fine. Similarly, you might call the three realms of Land, Sea, and Sky from Celtic tradition. For an example of an opening that uses the four elements, consider "Circle Casting Song" by Susan Falkenrath Wolf on *Second Chants*. Here is a very simple circle casting I wrote for a Yule ritual, in which we handed a lit candle from person to person:

> As the flickering light is passed
> Hand to hand the circle is cast.

For an example of a closing, consider "Merry Meet" (also known as "May the Circle Be Open") recorded on *Songs of the Sacred Wheel*.

In order to write good openings and closings, you need to think of them as a frame. The opening expands your mind and gets the magic started. Therefore, openings need to be energetic and uplifting. The closing completes what the opening began, restoring everything to ordinary. Therefore, closings need to be solid and affirming. Together they support and contain the rest of the ritual. Look to doors, windows, and gates for inspiration.

When brainstorming ideas for a set of openings and closings, seek pairs of ideas that you can divide. For instance, in a ritual set on a beach, your opening might mention the tide coming in, and the closing would mention the tide going out. Divide a page in half, then write "start" and "finish" at the top, and see how many words you can associate with each. Pull out your tables of correspondence and look up associated symbols too.

If your composition addresses someone in particular, such as a guardian spirit or the members of a coven, it helps to name them early on. (Follow this up by mentioning the same names in the closing, to maintain balance.) State what you want to accomplish. Wrap up the composition with a clear conclusion. There are many traditional conclusions for openings (such as "Hail and well met!") and closings (such as "Merry part!") that you can use. In a group ritual, it adds power to have one person read the opening or closing, and the rest of the participants echo the last line. Plan accordingly.

Songs and Stories

Songs and stories are both forms of *narrative* in their most common ritual usage. They tell tales with magical or spiritual significance. The right one can suggest a theme and outline for an entire ritual.

Songs work a little bit differently than spoken words in ritual. (Ritual poems can also be declaimed rather than spoken or sung—declaiming sounds about halfway between the two.) Songs are often performed by a group of people working together, particularly with instrumental accompaniment. They customarily have a tune or rhythm, which is as much a part of the performance as the words. Songs can be used for raising power as well as directing the flow of magic. They work especially well when combined with other activities—for example, people may sing while dancing, making reverent gestures, passing a chalice around the circle, and so forth.

Songs may have a musical accompaniment, or be for voice(s) only. (Musical composition lies outside the scope of this book; we're just going to touch on the words.) There are even tunes that have multiple sets of lyrics to them. If you can't invent new tunes, choose a traditional tune and just write your own words to it, then include a note under the title citing which tune you used. Songs almost always rhyme, and they need a strong rhythm to carry the words along.

Songs consist of multiple verses, so they are harder to learn quickly than other forms of ritual poetry. They serve more for performance than participation, in most cases. However, if everyone knows the song, there is no reason why they can't join in. Thoughtful songwriters often include a chorus or a repeated line that an audience can learn quickly and sing along with, leaving the main singer(s) to do the rest of the verses alone. Of course, in a solitary ritual, you don't have to worry about other singers, or even how sweet your own voice may sound. Just sing for the joy and power of it. For an audio example, consider "The Witch Song" on *Circle Round and Sing* by Anne Hill. Here is a song in text:

"Morning" by Haroutune Toumanian

Day dawned. Bright tongues of scarlet flame
Shot up into the sky,
The livid heav'ns blushed, and became
A sea of crimson dye.

The sun his fiery beams unrolled
Like strands of coloured thread;
Embroidered all the clouds with gold,
And blue, and green, and red.

Then o'er the mountain, full in view,
Nature's great Monarch rose:

And from his tent of Royal blue
Hurled darts upon his foes.

Eternal foe of Gloom and Night,
On high he raised his arm;
His shield of gold, all shining bright,
Sheltered the world from harm.

To write good songs, you need a sense of exposition. Introduce the plot early on. Set the scene and describe the characters, then get them moving. Develop ideas as the song progresses. Create some tension and then resolve it. End with a flourish.

In songs, more than other ritual poetry, you also need an ear for the lyrical sound of language. Word choice carries a great deal of weight. Your phrases should spin themselves out effortlessly and beautifully, a delight to sing and to hear. So think of things that build and swell and take your breath away: a glorious sunrise, a rose blossoming, the arrival of a thunderstorm, sledding downhill, the ignition of a fire.

Stories add drama to ritual. Historical evidence suggests that the earliest plays were sacred theater: myths, legends, and other folklore acted out before an audience. Today, this type of performance remains an important inspiration for rituals, especially public ones presented in front of large crowds.

A story may be told by one person, or by several people each acting as a different character. Costumes and props add to the theatrical impact. Occasionally the audience may play a role, making gestures or sound effects. Similar to a song, a story can suggest the framework for an entire ritual, or it can be added for emphasis into an existing ritual whose theme it matches. However, a story offers more flexibility than a song because the speaker controls the pace, volume, and embellishments instead of being stuck with a specific tune and lyrics.

Here is an example from Cherokee mythology:

"The Milky Way" by James Mooney

Some people in the south had a corn mill, in which they pounded the corn into meal, and several mornings when they came to fill it they noticed that some of the meal had been stolen during the night. They examined the ground and found the tracks of a dog, so the next night they watched, and when the dog came from the north and began to eat the meal out of the bowl they sprang out and whipped him. He ran off howling to his home in the north, with the meal dropping from his mouth as he ran, and leaving behind a white trail where now we see the Milky Way, which the Cherokee call to this day *Gi'li'-utsûñ'stänûñ'yi,* "Where the dog ran."

This story would fit into several types of ritual. It could raise power for catching a thief, teach people about Dog as an animal guide, celebrate Cherokee culture, or honor the stars and the night sky. Each of those would emphasize a different aspect of the story, but for all of them you might have people dressed as the villagers and the dog, or paint a backdrop of a starry sky, and serve cornbread for the "Cakes and Ale" portion of ritual.

To tell an effective story, you need four things: theme, characters, setting, and plot. The theme conveys what the story is "about"—life, death, love, talent, tragedy, and so on. The characters are the people in the story. The setting is where things happen, and the plot is what goes on in the story. In the previous example, the theme is the origin of the Milky Way, the characters are the people and the dog, and the plot is the dog's theft of the cornmeal. The setting is not tightly specified, but it does range from south to north, as the dog runs away.

Deciding what kind of story you want to tell usually gives you its theme. Then ask yourself what kind of people (and they can be humans, gods or goddesses, animals, or any other figures that seem right) would have something important to say about that theme. Put them in a logical place—kings in a palace, priestesses in a temple, animals in a forest—and get them into some trouble. The trouble is the plot, and when they get themselves out of the trouble (or not), that's the resolution, and you're all done.

You can use many of the literary techniques in creating your story, but keep them subtle. Rhyme and meter make a poem or song, not a story, so avoid those here. Kennings, epithets, and other name-related tricks highlight the important people and things. Repeated phrases make great mnemonics; maybe the hero is always "stout as a house," or the coveted object of a quest is "the coal-black cauldron of birth." This makes it easier for you to remember the story, and easier for the audience to follow it. Use short words and simple sentences to speed up the pace; use long, fancy words and complicated sentences to slow things down. Build the tension and excitement to a high climax and then resolve it in a quick swoop to the conclusion.

Invocations, Evocations, and Devocations

Together, these compositions regulate the passage of incorporeal entities into and out of sacred space. Invocations and evocations invite a particular guardian spirit, elemental, patron deity, or other entity to participate in a ritual. Invocations bring the summoned entity into a person's body and mind. Evocations bring the summoned entity into the circle at large, or into a magical vessel such as a statue or jar. Both methods work, but the invocation tends to demand more of the person. Devocations release a summoned entity back to its usual home.

Invocations, evocations, and devocations may be rhymed or unrhymed, long or short. Many of the best ones are rather long and unrhymed, yet have a spoken rhythm that helps carry the speaker through them. The more complicated and powerful the entity you want to summon, the longer and more detailed you should make your summons. A devocation should match the style of invocation or evocation it reverses. It may be a little shorter, but not so much as to seem abrupt.

In composing summons, be as specific as possible. Describe the entity addressed by name, title(s), and attributes. This helps prevent mishaps such as the wrong entity answering. Invocations and evocations should also describe what the ritual is about, and what the speaker would like the entity to do, such as enter the circle or speak through the High Priestess. Always invite, never coerce! Many invocations and evocations begin with the entity's name or title, and end with a reference to that entity being present. For instance, consider "Herne Who Hears" by Ivo Dominguez Jr. on *A Dream Whose Time Is Coming*.

To write good invocations and evocations, you need to think of the composition as a sort of funnel. If you build it correctly, it will direct the summoned entity into the appropriate vessel, whether this is a person or an object. But if you're careless with your composition or delivery, the funnel won't work properly; it will "spill" magic all over—and that is as unpleasant as splashing water all over your clothes, or worse. Look for imagery that conveys a sense of travel and destination, flow and focus; think of horses, arrows, magnifying glasses, or rivers.

To write good devocations, you need to complement the prior invocation or evocation. They should balance each other the way that ritual openings and closings do. Name the entity, thank it for its assistance, and release it to go back to its point of origin. If your ritual is on the short and simple side, then devocations can be shortened in comparison to invocations or evocations. If your ritual is long and intense, don't skimp on the devocations because people will need time for a gradual return to ordinary consciousness, and this is an important step in that process.

Here is a matched pair of invocation and devocation in prose:

"Great Mother Invocation and Devocation"
by Elizabeth Barrette

Great Mother, bountiful goddess of all life, hear me now. I stand in the circle, between here and there, between past and future, balanced in all ways. By my belly and my breasts, I call to you. By the warmth of my womanhood, I call to you. By magic ancient and yet forever new, I call to you. Fill me now and speak to those assembled. So mote it be!

Great Mother, bountiful goddess of all life, hear me now. You have filled me with your boundless power and shared your wisdom with those gathered near. We thank you for all you have given us. Arise now and return to your true abode. Hail and farewell!

These could be used by a priestess in any ritual in which the celebrants desired to speak with the Great Mother. They would work especially well in an esbat, or in sabbats during the warm seasons when the Earth is alive and growing.

Activities

Rituals need to include more than just words, or they wind up with a "talking heads" problem. Plan to involve the body as well as the mind. This often means writing out the activities, both for people's bodies and for any tools or supplies used, similar to stage directions in a play. There are many activities useful in rituals: dancing, standing up, sitting down, walking in a circle, holding hands, and so on. Most of these are familiar and need little description. However, there are also activities unique to ritual performance; most magical and spiritual traditions have some of their own, and others are widespread.

Body Postures

Body postures are special arrangements of the legs, arms, and body. They may represent or honor summoned entities, focus power, signify mood, and so forth. Many sacred postures have names, which makes them easy to write about; it's simpler to say "Assume the Goddess posture" than to say "Stand up straight, with your feet shoulder-width apart, and your arms raised above your head to form a V-shape." This adds strong visual and tactile components to a Goddess invocation, and other postures similarly suggest their own uses. For illustrations and descriptions of some body postures often appearing in rituals, see *Ways of the Strega: Italian Witchcraft* by Raven Grimassi, and *Grimoire for the Apprentice Wizard* by Oberon Zell-Ravenheart.

Symbolic Actions

Symbolic actions are related to body postures, but they incorporate motion. They also have a more precise application, whereas body postures can serve various purposes. The motions facilitate specific magical and spiritual effects. For example, "The Great Rite" in symbol involves lowering an athame (usually held by a man) into a chalice (usually held by a woman) to represent sexual union of male and female, god and goddess. "Drawing Down the Moon" has variations across traditions, but generally features a motion from moon to woman, so that the goddess may speak through her. The serving of "Cakes and Ale" entails the sharing of food and drink (not necessarily cake and ale, specifically), and is a Pagan analog of the holy communion performed in Christian churches. It facilitates spiritual communion, and also helps people reconnect with their physical bodies after magical exercise. Each of these symbolic actions can become the heart of a ritual, holding a great deal of power.

Salutes

Salutes are combinations of words and motions that indicate respect and reverence. These appear in rites of passage, and often in other rituals when two or more people colead the celebration. Among the most famous is the Wiccan "Fivefold Kiss," in which a priest kisses a priestess on the feet, knees, genitals, breast, and lips (or vice versa with a priestess kissing a priest) while reciting a blessing. Another is the Hindi salute "Namaste," the spoken word accompanied by a bow, with the palms pressed together in front of the chest. It means "The god/dess in me greets the god/dess in you."

If you belong to an established tradition, do some research on what kind of body postures, symbolic actions, and salutes it features. If you follow an eclectic or solitary path, devise your own ritual activities. For inspiration, consider the symbolism of numbers, geometric shapes, directions, runes, and other sigils, which you could somehow embody. Look at pictures or statues of deities, animals, and other spiritual figures to see how you might mimic their poses or shapes. Children's songs and games also offer examples of symbolic motions. Read a few scripts of plays to get a sense of how to write stage directions for actions. Don't be afraid to experiment— move your body in ritual and explore what feels right for you.

These compositions and activities make up the basic parts of a ritual. Other types of composition discussed in previous chapters may also appear. In the next chapter, we'll take a look at how these pieces fit together to form a whole ritual.

Exercises

Use these exercises to practice composing ritual parts. You may pick and choose, or do the whole set. It's a good idea to mix these with exercises from previous chapters, as ritual parts can take many different forms. Also consider repeating them, slanting your work toward different types of ritual.

Exercise #1: Squaring the Circle

If you attend a ritual at a festival, chances are it will include "casting the circle," with participants standing in a ring. However, nothing says that every ritual group must form a circle! Compose a matched opening and closing for a ritual in which everyone stands in a square.

Exercise #2: From Song to Ceremony

Reread the song "Morning" earlier in this chapter. Briefly outline a ritual using this song as the focus.

Exercise #3: Telling Our Stories

You have been asked to lead a coming-of-age ritual for a young person who looks up to you. This person loves myths, folklore, and storytelling. Come up with a story that matches the topic of the ritual. You may choose a traditional story and retell it in your own words, or compose one from scratch.

Exercise #4: Yule Log Rescue

This evocation is meant to be read by the High Priest while the High Priestess kindles the Yule Log in their fireplace. The High Priest wrote it in a hurry, so it needs a lot of revision. Help him straighten it out.

On the longest nite,

The Dark the and Light do battle.

Through the winter is far from over,

The Light is victorious drives out the Dark.

We call upon the fire before me

To aide the Light, in this quest.

Blazin flames of Yule,

Leap forth from the hearth!

Consumate the YuleLog

As the Light consumes the Darkness!

We throw the Ule Log on the hearth
And summon the sacred flame!
By Bel, by Loki, by Hephaestus,
So mote it be!

Exercise #5: Pairing Up

Reread the "Great Mother" matched pair of invocation and devocation earlier in this chapter. Now write a similar pair for a deity or other higher power—preferably one you work with regularly—of your choice.

Exercise #6: Mirror and Music

For this exercise, you will need a mirror (as large as possible), a sound system of some kind, and an album of whatever sacred music you enjoy. Arrange the mirror so that you can see yourself clearly. Start the music. Listen for a little while and let the music bring you into a sacred state of consciousness.

Begin to move with the music. Don't worry about trying to dance or do anything specific, just let the sounds guide your body. As you move, watch the mirror so you can see how your motions look. Watch for poses or moves that are evocative and eye-catching. Repeat your favorites, and keep watching for new ones. Do this for 10 minutes or so.

Afterward, write down descriptions of the poses or moves that you liked the best, and imagine how you might incorporate them into a ritual. You may want to doodle a picture of the pose or move to give you a visual reference too.

Chapter Eleven: Writing Wonderful Rituals—The Process

Writing shapes all stages of a ritual. It creates the framework and the individual components. Thus far we've explored many different types of magical composition useful in ritual. (If you have skipped around previously, make sure you've covered everything. This chapter requires familiarity with knowledge and skills presented in all the earlier chapters.) Now we're going to examine the process of ritual design and what goes into making an effective, memorable, and safe ritual.

Beyond the compositions themselves lie some other concerns that go into ritual design. These include the size of the ritual, its magical aspects, and its presentation. That's a lot to think about, but you can do it. All the practice you've done with shorter compositions will make ritual design more manageable for you.

Putting It All Together

Although rituals vary greatly in detail, an underlying structure exists. They all have a beginning, a middle, and an end. Within those sections, certain options appear, depending on the tradition and the purpose. The exact order is somewhat flexible. Here is an outline of a generic Pagan ritual, which can adapt to most traditions and purposes.

Generic Ritual Outline
I. Beginning
   A. Site preparation
   B. Participant preparation
   C. Establishment of sacred/magical space
II. Main Body
   A. Statement of intent
   B. Invocation or evocation of higher power(s)
   C. Ritual drama or other celebration
   D. Activity to raise power
   E. Activity to release power toward desired goal
   F. "Cakes and Ale" or other communion
III. Ending
   A. Devocation of higher power(s)
   B. Return of sacred/magical space to ordinary
   C. Cleanup

In some ways, ritual design follows much the same pattern as the other types of writing described in earlier chapters. You begin with a theme or goal of some kind, and also jot down some ideas branching out from there. Rough in an outline of what you'd like to do. Then you do research, which fleshes out your early ideas and generates new ones. Using this material, write out the individual parts of the ritual such as the opening, invocation or evocation of higher powers, and so forth. Add descriptive stage directions where needed to tie everything together.

As an example, let's work with a Midsummer theme. A Midsummer ritual might make you think of the sun, fire, growth, and solar deities. Brainstorm to develop these broad ideas into specific activities; for instance, "sun" might lead to using sunflower seed cakes and sun tea for Cakes and Ale.

Next, narrow down the possibilities generated by brainstorming. You might select motifs belonging to a single tradition for harmony, or combine motifs from different traditions for diversity. In this case, choosing the archetypal "Sun God" and "Earth Goddess" makes the ritual accessible to a wide range of participants, such as the members of an eclectic coven.

Now, plug these ideas into the generic outline to create a working outline for this ritual:

Midsummer Ritual Outline

   I. Beginning
      A. Prepare the site
      B. Purify participants as they arrive
      C. Cast circle using sunflower seeds
      D. Call the Quarters with summer imagery

  II. Main Body
      A. Summarize the ritual's content and goal
      B. High Priest evokes Sun God
      C. High Priestess evokes Earth Goddess
      D. Chant to raise power
      E. High Priest uses a magnifying glass to light a small fire
      F. High Priestess blesses the fertile season
      G. "Cakes and Ale" using sunflower seed cakes and sun tea

 III. Ending
      A. Devoke the Earth Goddess
      B. Devoke the Sun God
      C. Release the Quarters
      D. Open the circle
      E. Extinguish fire and clean up site

Thus for a whole ritual, you first block out the structure to show the beginning, middle, and end, including any specific things you want in each place. Then you pick the types of composition best suited to the structure of the ritual and the goal you have set. Possibilities include poems, chants, prayers, blessings, openings and closings, invocations and devocations, songs, and stories. Take extra care to distinguish where you may need multiple parts—it's easy to ruin a ritual by trying to cram what should be two or three activities into one. If you start writing and your composition tries to pull itself into separate pieces, maybe you should let it.

To keep this simple, let's go through our Midsummer ritual one section at a time. The beginning needs setup instructions, purification, and circle casting in addition to the Quarter calls. Couplets will make a short and sweet set of Quarter calls. Together we wind up with:

Preparation: Set up an outdoor altar with sunflower seeds, magnifying glass, fireproof bowl full of tinder, sunflower seed cakes, and sun tea. High Priest wears yellow for the sun; High Priestess wears green for the Earth. Coveners gather at the edge of what will become sacred space.

Purification: One at a time, coveners step forward. High Priest greets them: "All that the light touches is pure. Nothing impure can stand in the light." They respond: "I stand in the light, unafraid and pure." Coveners move to form a ring around the altar. High Priest and High Priestess purify each other last, then join the ring.

Cast Circle: High Priestess scatters the sunflower seeds in a wide circle, enclosing the coven and the altar, and visualizing a protective barrier.

Call Quarters: As each of the four callers delivers their lines, the coveners turn to face that direction.

> From the East I call the warm morning breeze
> To lift our minds and whisper in the trees
>
> From the South I call the bright sun of noon
> To quicken our hearts and ripen crops soon

> From the West I call the afternoon rain
> To quench our souls' thirst and water the plain
>
> From the North I call the rich earth of night
> To bear our bodies and temper the light

The middle of the ritual contains multiple parts. The statement of intent is often improvised, so we can let the High Priestess ad lib that. It leads nicely into free verse evocations for the Sun God and Earth Goddess. For a chant, we want something with strong rhythm and rhyme, such as short couplets. At the peak of power, the High Priest will manifest the sun's energy by starting a fire, which we can simply describe. For the High Priestess's blessing, we'll use free verse again, as too many different forms in a single ritual can get confusing. (Refer back to earlier chapters for details on forms.) The communion needs only a brief description.

Statement of Intent: High Priestess improvises a few words about the meaning of Midsummer, touching on the summer solstice and life at its peak.

Evocation of Sun God: High Priest raises his hands and says:

> I call the divine masculine in His guise as the Sun,
>
> Giver of life and light, lord of all above.
>
> Today is Midsummer, the longest day of the year,
>
> When His power reaches its peak.
>
> Sun God, join us in our circle now.
>
> Hail and well met!
>
> [Coveners repeat] Hail and well met!

Evocation of Earth Goddess: High Priestess raises her hands and says:

> I call the divine feminine in Her guise as the Earth,
>
> Our verdant and fertile mother, lady of all below.
>
> At the height of the growing season

She turns the Sun's power into fruit and flesh.

Earth Goddess, rise up to meet us here.

Hail and well met!

[Coveners repeat] Hail and well met!

Chant: The coven's best vocalist leads everyone in the chant.

Earth and Sun

Well begun

Sun and Earth

Growth and birth

Ritual Drama: High Priest listens to the chant and gauges when it is near the peak of power. Then he uses a magnifying glass to focus solar energy into the bowl, igniting the tinder there. When the flames appear, the chant stops and everyone thrusts their hands inward, pushing the power into the bowl.

Blessing: High Priestess delivers the blessing, using the solar/fire energy to empower it.

The Sun God sends His light and heat to us.

May He bless us to shine from within;

May He bless the world to flourish.

The Earth Goddess brings forth Her bounty.

May She bless us to nourish each other;

May She bless the land with abundance.

As the fire burns, may the blessing go forth

With its radiance to touch us and the world around.

Blessed be!

[Coveners repeat] Blessed be!

Cakes and Ale: High Priest carries a platter of sunflower seed cakes around the circle so that everyone may partake. High Priestess follows with a chalice of sun tea. They serve each other last, then return the items to the altar.

For the conclusion, we need devocations for the Earth Goddess and Sun God, which should match the free verse evocations. We also need to release the Quarters, which should match the couplets used in the calls and proceed in reverse order. Add a few words to open the circle, then tidy up loose ends, and we're done.

Devocation of Earth Goddess: High Priestess raises her hands and says:

> I give honor to the Earth Goddess
> For meeting us here in our circle
> And bringing Her fertile power.
> Return with our thanks to the infinite below.
> Hail and farewell!
>
> [Coveners repeat] Hail and farewell!

Devocation of Sun God: High Priest raises his hands and says:

> I give honor to the Sun God
> For joining our ritual today
> And bringing His radiant glory.
> Return with our thanks to the infinite above.
> Hail and farewell!
>
> [Coveners repeat] Hail and farewell!

Release Quarters: As each of the four callers delivers his or her lines, the coveners turn to face that direction.

> In the North I release the deep, dark Earth
> With thanks for sharing your infinite worth
>
> In the West I release the rain, and soon
> With thanks we conclude our circle this June
>
> In the South I release the brilliant sun
> With thanks for doing the work that you've done
>
> In the East I release the breeze, and so
> With thanks for our breath, it is time to go.

Open Circle: High Priestess says, "The circle is open, but unbroken." Everyone responds, "Merry meet, and merry part, and merry meet again!"

Cleanup: High Priest extinguishes the fire if it has not burned out yet. Once cool, the ashes should be scattered upon the Earth. Coveners dismantle the altar setup and put things away. High Priestess makes sure the ritual site is fully restored to its original condition.

So, this is how a ritual comes together, from idea to outline to complete draft. At this stage you can compare it to your goal and perhaps tinker with it a bit, before you move on to revision (which we'll discuss shortly).

As you write your ritual, and especially as you look at your draft, consider the context and logistics. Do you plan to hold the ritual outdoors or indoors—or does it need to work in either setting, in case the location changes on short notice? You don't want to write "feel the sun on your face" for a ritual held indoors or at night! What will the temperature be like? Make sure that any costumes called for in the ritual match the comfort level. Also, although a huge bonfire feels great on a cool spring or autumn evening, it may overheat people in summer. What tools or supplies may support the words? If you have access to a real cauldron for a Samhain ritual, take advantage of that by writing a description of it into your opening or invocation. Work as much of this into your text as you comfortably can, to provide subtle and effective guidance for participants.

It's okay to try different things and swap pieces around until you're happy with the results. Just because you start out with a myth in the middle, doesn't mean you can't change your mind and retell it in a song, move it closer to the beginning or end, or substitute something else entirely. Ultimately, aim for cohesion, so that the individual parts form a greater whole and the sequence makes sense.

Many books and Websites contain complete rituals for you to use as examples, such as *Dancing with the Sun: Celebrating the Seasons of Life* by Yasmine Galenorn or "The Cauldron: A Pagan Forum" online.[1] Further advice on ritual design per se is harder to find. Two resources worth tracking down are *Ritual Craft* by Amber K and Azrael Arynn K, and *Rites of Worship: A Neopagan Approach* by Isaac Bonewits.

Polishing Your Ritual

Revision depth depends on the complexity of the composition. Simple compositions such as those discussed earlier—blessings, chants, and so forth—are fairly straightforward to revise. Something as complicated as a ritual, which includes a number of component parts that must all work together, takes more. In such cases, it helps to revise your work in stages.

The first round of revision should focus on relatively large-scale aspects of writing. Does the organization make sense and flow smoothly? If not, you may need to add things, move things, or strengthen the sequencing cues. Is the tone consistent and appropriate to the topic? Handfasting rituals should sound loving and festive, blessings should sound reverent, openings should sound welcoming, and so forth. Are the activities safe? You may need to modify some or add precautions. Does the composition generally meet your goals and expectations? If not, it will be easier to make major changes now, before you invest further time and energy into more detailed polishing.

The middle round(s) of revision should focus on a smaller scale. Now that you've fixed any large-scale problems, you can concentrate on such things as word choice and pacing. An excellent way to accomplish this is to read your composition out loud. This is optional for something intended for use only as text, such as a prayer that you will write on parchment paper and throw into the fire. If you or someone else will be reading your composition aloud during a ritual, then you really need to make sure that it *works* as spoken or sung material. Sometimes things that look good on paper don't sound good when pronounced, or cause your tongue to trip over them. Fix these glitches by reordering words and phrases, or by choosing words with a different number of syllables or different sounds.

Tighten your writing. Delete redundant words.

Check magical aspects with care. Rituals customarily include symmetrical actions: A circle is cast and later released, an entity is invoked or evoked and later devoked. Make sure that your composition undoes everything it does, except for those aspects intended to remain in effect after the ritual concludes. For all types of magical writing, check the wording to confirm that everything you have said is something you want to be true or to happen. If you talk about "rains of renewal" in an Ostara chant, you are likely to get wet!

This is a good time to ask someone else to read your draft in progress and provide feedback. Make changes as needed, at each round of revision. Repeat until you feel largely satisfied with this version. If practical, set the composition aside for a few days before you do the final round.

The last round of revision involves proofreading. Now you're down to the tiny little details of spelling and punctuation. Watch for common typos such as "teh" for "the." If you write with a word processor, use the spellcheck function, but don't rely solely on it. (Software can't always tell whether you should use "by," "bye," or "buy," for example.) Follow up with human-eye proofreading. If you work on paper, you'll need to proofread the old-fashioned way anyhow. Make sure that every sentence begins with a capital letter and ends with a punctuation mark. Correct any mistakes involving commas, quotation marks, or other punctuation.

Finally, proofread for formatting. If you're writing a ritual with several subsections, they need to match. You may italicize all the stage directions for physical actions, or you may indent prose readings differently from chants or poems. Whatever formatting you choose, keep it consistent, so that your finished ritual looks elegant.

Ritual design is the most complicated of the compositions presented in this book, and for that reason, one of the more challenging to write. If you feel overwhelmed, try breaking it down into its component pieces. You might also backtrack to an earlier chapter and practice individual compositions some more, before returning to the complex ones. The more you practice writing, the better you get. Don't be afraid to stretch yourself—a good ritual is worth all the effort you put into it, creating memories that can last a lifetime.

Exercises

Use these exercises to practice overall ritual design and assembly. You may do just a few of them, or work your way through the whole set. This is also a good time to go back and do exercises from previous chapters, as most of them feed into this process.

Exercise #1: Your Favorite Ritual

Think back to the best ritual you can recall. What was its theme? What kinds of compositions did it include? What were the activities? Was it a solitary, coven, or public ritual? Briefly describe the original ritual. Then adapt it for the other two modes; for instance, turning a coven ritual into a solitary ritual and a public ritual.

Exercise #2: Sounding Off

Attend a ritual; if you can't find one of your own tradition, you may substitute another magical or spiritual event. Pay careful attention to the speakers. How do they sound? Can you hear them clearly? How much power do their voices have? Look at the way they hold their bodies. Do they stand still, or do they move around and make gestures? When you get home, repeat as much of the ritual language as you can remember (and as much as seems safe, if the content was intense). Duplicate the volume, tone, and delivery of the original as best you can.

Exercise #3: Your Magical Abilities

What are your skills and talents? How could you employ them in a ritual? Make a list of at least five things you can do. For each, give at least two ways you could use it in a ritual context.

Exercise #4: Describing Energy

Attend a magical or spiritual ritual; it doesn't have to belong to your own tradition. Pay close attention to the ambient energy, and to the way it rises, falls, flows, and otherwise changes through the course of the ritual. Afterward, describe the energy as precisely as you can. Be creative, play with words, try out different imagery. How would you talk about energy within the text of a ritual? Give at least three examples.

Exercise #5: Rejoice in the Sun

Reread the two ritual outlines under "Putting It All Together." Adapt them into a complete ritual text for celebrating Midsummer at a large festival. To personalize this ritual, modify it from the Midsummer example by choosing individual deities instead of archetypes, and switch from evocation to invocation. You may change other details if you wish.

Exercise #6: Saving a Rainy Day

Imagine that you have arranged to lead the ritual from Exercise #5—but alas! An hour before the scheduled start time, a summer thunderstorm deluges your location. A crowd of dripping, disappointed people are looking to you for guidance. Rewrite your ritual for indoor use—and do it in 20 minutes or less. Time yourself. Sometimes real life demands quick work.

Exercise #7: Outline Revision

A friend of yours is writing a Croning ritual for a Celtic circle of older women. She has asked you to look over her outline. It needs some work. Correct the problems that you find.

Celtic Croning Ritual Outline

I. Beginning
   A. Cast the circle
   B. Purify participants
   C. Call the Celtic Realms of Land, Sea, and Sky

II. Main Body
   A. Statement of intent
   B. Priestess invokes Hecate
   C. Spiral dance to raise power
   D. Priestess/Hecate welcomes the new Crone and bestows a violet cloak
   E. "Cakes and ale"

III. Ending
   A. Devoke Hecate
   B. Open the circle
   C. Clean up the site

Chapter Twelve: Sharing Your Work

Literature began as a spoken art, not a written one. *Oral tradition* predates written compositions by thousands of years. Some of the greatest material that survives today was originally oral tradition, recorded long after its creation. Bards, skalds, Griots, cantastories, troubadours—specialists of many names, in many countries, served their people by memorizing and reciting vast repertoires of lore.[1] Historic cultures placed great importance on these matters. A storyteller or poet sometimes held status equal to that of a king!

So hold your head up. You belong to a grand tradition. Part of that entails learning how to share your work with other people in an effective and exciting manner. If you choose to make a habit of performance, your skills will increase in time. If you choose to keep your activities private, well, writing for just yourself will seem easy in comparison to reading before an audience! A third option is to share your work from a distance, by submitting it for publication.

The Role of Writing in Paganism

The field of Pagan nonfiction and fiction dates back many years, including such early gems as *Aradia: The Gospel of the Witches* (1890) by Charles Leland. Many Pagan scholars begin the modern era with the works of Gerald Gardner: *High Magic's Aid* (1949), *The Gardnerian Book of Shadows* (around 1953), *Witchcraft Today* (1954), and *The Meaning of Witchcraft*

(1959). During the 1960s and especially the 1970s, books about magic and Paganism were few and hard to find, but this period brought many of the best and most famous titles: *The Golden Ass* translated by Jack Lindsay (1960), *Natural Magic* by Doreen Valiente (1975), *When God Was a Woman* by Merlin Stone (1976), *Drawing Down the Moon* by Margot Adler (1979), and *The Spiral Dance* by Starhawk (1979). Selection and distribution continued to grow throughout the 1980s, and by the 1990s there came a tremendous expansion as people who had grown up on those earlier books began to write their own. Today most bookstores have a shelf, and often a whole case or two, of Pagan/magical/occult titles.

To a large extent, that publishing boom fueled the rise of the contemporary Pagan and magical movement as a culture. For most of history, these things remained much more localized; seekers had to track down obscure texts or reclusive practitioners in order to learn much. Now information is readily available, not just in books but also through the Internet, which of course is another manifestation of writing.

What used to be chiefly oral tradition has come to rely more on written transmission, making it accessible to almost everyone. With that growth have come festivals that revive the oral transmission, in a neverending cycle. Together, these two aspects of our culture create ever more opportunities to explore ourselves and each other. From small coven spells to huge public rituals, from books to Weblogs, writing has more impact when shared with an audience.

The book you're holding now is part of my contribution to this cultural tide. What will yours be? That's up to you. Here are some more ideas to explore....

If You Want to Get Published

Much magical and spiritual writing is produced for personal use. It never travels beyond the writer's own hands, or at most those of friends and covenmates. Some people, however, want to share their work with a wider audience—or even make a career of writing for pay. It's not terribly difficult to get your work printed in a small-circulation newsletter or on a Website. Getting published in a major Pagan, New Age, or other magical market poses more of a challenge. Preparing a composition for market, and finding the right home for it, takes some extra work. However, it also brings tremendous rewards. If this appeals to you, here are some things you can do to improve your chances of success.

If at all possible, share your rough draft with some friends and get their feedback. These are your *first readers*. They will see things in your work—good and bad—that you haven't seen. Let them know that you want their *honest* opinion, not just ego stroking. Honesty will serve you better in developing your skills as a magical writer. Do you know a secretary or an English teacher? Such people make excellent first readers, especially for proofreading. Do you know other writers? You may arrange to trade *critiques* of each other's work, detailing what worked and what didn't work in a composition. Most writers do well with one to three first readers. Prolific writers may need more.

With luck, you might even find a writer's group in your area. Such groups meet regularly to critique each other's work. Not only will you get experienced feedback on your own writing, but you will also have the chance to analyze other people's writing—and that improves your own revision skills. This is useful in any case, but especially if you aspire to publishing your work, if you plan to do a lot of writing, or if you like the idea of designing large public rituals.

Suppose that you can't find any first readers or writer's groups in your area. Don't worry, feedback doesn't have to happen in person. You can e-mail your writing to friends in far away places for their input. Also, many writer's groups exist online in various formats, including e-mail lists, chat groups, and Website forums. Look for one that focuses on nonfiction, poetry, magical composition, or whatever your specialty is. Alternatively, find a general group that discusses all types of writing; this works whether you've got a specialty that you can't find a group to match, or you write many different types of material. Of course, you could also *start* a writer's group of your own.

When you receive a critique of your work, first thank the person for their time and input. Then consider the feedback in detail. Remember that you don't have to use *every* suggestion that you receive. Some should prove useful, but others probably will not. Use your best judgment; after all, it's your composition. A good rule of thumb is that you can ignore an observation made by one person, if you have a valid reason for doing so. You should give extra thought to anything mentioned by two different people. If three or more people make the same complaint—especially if they didn't talk to each other, but noticed it independently—then they are almost certainly right, even if you disagree with them.

Also, consider the source. Place more weight on comments from people whose opinions you respect, or whose mastery of language, poetry, spellcraft, ritual design, or magical lore you admire. Don't take negative feedback too personally; it's rarely meant that way. Don't let flattery go to your head, either; it may be sincere, but that doesn't mean there's no room for improvement.

Bear in mind a few basic guidelines for commenting on other people's work: Read when you have the time and energy to give the material your full attention. Keep notes as you go along, particularly tracking anything that jolts you out of the text. Mix criticism of flaws with praise of what works. Be as specific as you can: "This ritual is stupid" is much less useful than "Mars is not really a god of love." If you can think of some, suggest ways to fix the problems you have identified. Avoid rude remarks; make your points gently if possible, firmly if necessary. Treat other writers and their works as you would wish to be treated.

Markets and Submissions

Once you've polished your composition, you need to decide on a market. There are many magazines, newsletters, webzines, and other places that publish magical/spiritual writing. Read a variety of these to learn what they print. Hardcopy market guides such as *Writer's Market* or *Poet's Market* give contact information and brief descriptions for hundreds of markets, updated annually. You can also hunt for markets using online resources, such as the searchable database maintained by Writers Write, Inc.

Make a list of the markets/publishers that seem to be a good match for your writing. Look up their submission guidelines online, or request a copy of their guidelines via postal mail. Then decide where to send your composition first. You may choose the "best" market based on highest pay, largest circulation, highest acceptance rate, or other criteria. Sort your list in that order. If the first publisher doesn't accept your composition, simply submit it to the next one on the list.

Next, you need to prepare your composition for submission by putting it into a manuscript format. *There is no single "standard manuscript format."* There are some common rules, and a lot of variation based on individual editor preferences; hence the importance of requesting and following guidelines for each specific market. Electronic submissions typically require an e-mail message with the manuscript either attached (as a Microsoft Word document, or a rich text file) or pasted directly as plain text. Hardcopy submissions should be printed with black ink on white paper, double-spaced on one side of the page, using a plain font such as Times New Roman or Arial. At the top of the first page, put your legal name, pen name if you use one, postal address, and e-mail address. For a more detailed look at manuscript format, consult a writing guide such as Mary Lynn's *Every Page Perfect*.

Submission method depends on mode. Electronic submissions are usually e-mailed to the editor. Some Websites have a form for submissions; just follow the instructions they give you. Hardcopy submissions should be mailed flat in a large envelope, with a self-addressed stamped envelope included for the reply. Include a cover letter with hardcopy submissions to introduce your manuscript, briefly summarize any publication credits or qualifications you may have, and thank the editors for their attention.

Finally, keep a record of what you submit where, and what happens to it. This will prevent you from sending a manuscript to the same publisher twice, or to two different publishers at the same time. (Most editors don't accept simultaneous submissions, so it's vital to submit a given manuscript to one publisher at a time.) An accurate record also helps in tracking your success rate.

Exercises

Use these exercises to explore ways of sharing your work with other people, at a distance and in person. You may pick and choose whichever ones seem interesting, or do all of these. This is also a good time to go back and do exercises from previous chapters.

Exercise #1: On the Shoulders of Giants

All writers draw some influence from those who have gone before. Who are your favorite authors of magical and spiritual material? List at least three. For each of those, explore the similarities and differences between their style and yours. Then pick one and write a composition in the "voice" of that author.

Exercise #2: Group Think

Investigate at least two writer's groups. Try to find ones with different parameters, such as one local and one online, or one specialized and one general. How big are they? What are their rules for participation? Would you like to join one? If so, which one and why? If not, why not? Journal your thoughts.

Exercise #3: Going to Market

Visit a large bookstore near you, whichever one has the best selection of periodicals. Look through the Pagan and New Age magazines, as well as others with similar magical and spiritual flavor. What kinds of material are they buying—spells, rituals, inspirational poetry, individual components such as blessings or invocations? What topics do they cover? Does anything in these magazines sound similar to what you write? If you find a good match for your work, it's a good idea to buy the magazine so that you can read the whole thing and request a copy of its submission guidelines.

Afterword:
Conclusions on Magical Composition

By this point, you have a good working knowledge of magical writing in general, its processes, tools, and techniques. You have familiarized yourself with several specific types of magical writing: poetry, spells, chants, prayers, blessings, and rituals. You can explore other types of writing in much the same way, as you discover things that intrigue you.

Moreover, you now understand something of the magic of creativity, along with ways of summoning and channeling it. You know some ways of sharing your work with other people, in person or in print. You have learned critical thinking to analyze your own and other people's compositions. The exercises have given you a basis of experience on which to build. Beyond this, it's mainly a matter of practice.

For further study, you have many options. Reuse the exercises; most of them will function more than just once. Many writing books and Websites contain interesting exercises too. The more you write, the more progress you will make in developing your skills. Also, read as much as you can, both ancient and modern material. They can inspire you and improve your understanding of what makes writing great.

On a more interactive approach, form a club with some friends and continue to critique each other's work. Take a writing class at a nearby school, library, or community center—to be fair, although some are excellent, others are worse than useless, so choose with care. Attend, perform, or organize events that promote magical writing such as public rituals, poetry readings, bardic circles, and mythic storytelling. These activities build your audience, encourage people to enjoy magical writing, and also enhance your presentation skills.

Words are magic, some of the oldest and purest and most potent in the world. They are the stuff of legends, the purview of heroes, Wizards, deities, and stranger creatures than you have probably encountered yet. They can kindle passion and topple kingdoms, lift the downtrodden or mock the mighty. When you perform your compositions in ritual, the very universe cocks an ear to listen. All you need in the way of a magic wand to channel this power is...a pencil. Write wisely.

Notes

Chapter One
1. Pennick, 28–29.
2. "The Skald of the Scandinavian Medieaval Ages."
3. Lott, "Keepers of History."

Chapter Two
1. The Writing Center, "Brainstorming."
2. Ibid.
3. Baer, "Pre-Writing Strategies."
4. Turner, "How to Improve Your Memory."
5. Terri Wilson, "A Cup of Creativi-tea: Brainstorming."
6. Nuwer, 51–81.
7. Khalsa, 30–41.
8. Drury, 9–24.
9. Khalsa, 22.
10. Nuwer, 126–141.

Chapter Three
1. Drury, 64.
2. Drury, 65.

Chapter Four
1. Myers and Wukasch, 147–149.
2. Catherine Wilson, "Poetry: The Forms and the History: Elegy."
3. Drury, 104–106.
4. Myers and Wukasch, 40–41.

Chapter Five
1. Myers and Wukasch, 4–5.
2. Drury, 106–110.
3. Bashô, haiku. No page listed.
4. Myers and Wukasch, 48, 199.
5. Drury, 126–131.
6. Drury, 131–134.

Chapter Seven
1. Yoga Insight, "Yoga Chants."
2. "Gregorian Chant," Wikipedia.

Chapter Eight
1. Freysfriend, "Freyja."
2. "Prayer and Sacrifice," Illustrated History of the Roman Empire.
3. Ibid.
4. "History of Roman Catholic Novena," Roman Catholic Prayers.
5. Spellwerx, "Number Correspondences."
6. Legge, "33" in Tao Te Ching.
7. Grainger, 35.

Chapter Eleven
1. Randall, "Sample Pagan Rituals."

Chapter Twelve
1. Manwaring, 148.

Bibliography

A.E. "Immortality." In *Anthology of Irish Verse*. Edited by Padraic Colum, 1922, 156. *www.bartleby.com/250/156.html* (accessed June 27, 2006).

Adler, Margot. *Drawing Down the Moon: Witches, Druids, Goddess Worshippers, and Other Pagans in America Today*. New York: Viking Press, 1979. Revised & Expanded edition, New York: Penguin, 1997.

"Amergin." Anonymous (date unknown). *The Oxford Book of English Mystical Verse*. Edited by Nicholson and Lee, 1917, 1. *www.bartleby.com/236/1.html* (accessed June 24, 2006).

Apuleius, Lucius. *The Golden Ass*. Translated by Jack Lindsay. Bloomington, Ind.: Indiana University Press, 1960.

Assembly of the Sacred Wheel and friends. *A Dream Whose Time Is Coming*. Georgetown, Del.: Assembly of the Sacred Wheel, 2001.

Baer, Dee. "Pre-Writing Strategies." University of Delaware. *www.english.udel.edu/dbaer/prewriting.html* (accessed January 30, 2007).

Bashô. Haiku. 1644–1694. *www.geocities.com/Tokyo/Island/5022/basho.html* (accessed July 20, 2006).

Besen, Linda. "Proofreader's and Editor's Symbols." University of Colorado at Boulder, 2002. *www.colorado.edu/Publications/styleguide/symbols.html* (accessed January 30, 2007).

Billings, William. "Africa." In *The Singing Master's Assistant*, 3rd edition. Boston, 1781. *www.cpdl.org/wiki/index.php/Africa_%28William_Billings%29* (accessed September 1, 2006).

Bonewits, Isaac. *Rites of Worship: A Neopagan Approach*. El Sobrante, Calif.: Earth Religions Press, 2003.

Breen, Nancy, and Erika O'Connell, eds. *Poet's Market 2007*. Cincinnati, Ohio: Writer's Digest Books, 2006.

Brewer, Robert Lee, ed. *Writer's Market 2007*. Cincinnati, Ohio: Writer's Digest Books, 2006.

Bridges, Sallie. "Excalibur." 1864. *www.lib.rochester.edu/CAMELOT/ SBExcal.htm* (accessed 6/26/06).

Carbery, Ethna. "The Shadow House of Lugh." In *Anthology of Irish Verse*. Edited by Padraic Colum, 1922, 62. *www.bartleby.com/250/ 62.html* (accessed June 27, 2006).

Carmichael, Alexander. *Carmina Gadelica: Hymns and Incantations (Ortha Nan Gaidheal) Volume I*. 1900. *www.sacred-texts.com/neu/ celt/cg1/cg1048.htm* (accessed October 10, 2006).

"Come Let Us All A-Maying Go." Early 18th century. Index to Rounds. *www.personal.umich.edu/ ∼ msmiller/rcatch15.html* (accessed September 1, 2006).

Connor, Kerri. *The Pocket Spell Creator: Magickal References at Your Fingertips*. Franklin Lakes, N.J.: New Page Books, 2003.

Conway, D.J. *Lord of Light and Shadow: The Many Faces of the God*. St. Paul, Minn.: Llewellyn Publications, 1997.

Cunningham, Scott. *Cunningham's Encyclopedia of Crystal, Gem, & Metal Magic*. St. Paul, Minn.: Llewellyn Publications, 2002.

226. *Cunningham's Encyclopedia of Magical Herbs*. St. Paul, Minn.: Llewellyn Publications, 2000.

Dickinson, Emily. "The Sea of Sunset." In *Poems by Emily Dickinson Series One*. Edited by Mabel Loomis Todd and T.W. Higginson. 1886.*www.poetseers.org/early_american_poets/ emily_dickinson_poems_nature/11* (July 11, 2006).

Dominguez Jr., Ivo. "Herne Who Hears." Georgetown, Del.: Assembly of the Sacred Wheel, 2001.

Drury, John. *Creating Poetry*. Cincinnati, Ohio: Writer's Digest Books, 1991.

Freysfriend, Thorunn. "Freyja." Midgard Web's Book of Lore. *www.thorshof.org/zfreya.htm* (accessed September 18, 2006).

Galenorn, Yasmine. *Dancing with the Sun: Celebrating the Seasons of Life*. St. Paul, Minn.: Llewellyn Publications, 1999.

Gardner, Gerald. *High Magic's Aid*. Michael Houghton, 1949. London: Pentacle Enterprises, 1999.

————. *The Gardnerian Book of Shadows.* Approximately 1953. *www.sacred-texts.com/pag/gbos/* (accessed December 1, 2006).

————. *Witchcraft Today.* Rider & Co., 1954. New York: Magickal Childe Inc., 1980.

————. *The Meaning of Witchcraft.* London: Aquarian Press, 1959.

Gillette, J. Michael. *Theatrical Design and Production: An Introduction to Scene Design and Construction, Lighting, Sound, Costume, and Makeup (5th edition).* Boston: McGraw-Hill College, 2004.

Grainger, Roger. *Peace Prayers from the World's Faiths.* Ropley, UK: O Books, 2006.

"Greensleeves." Anonymous (sometimes alleged to be written by King Henry VIII of England, 1500s). In *A Handful of Pleasant Delites* by Clement Robinson and Divers Others, 1584. *http://whitewolf.newcastle.edu.au/words/authors/T/Traditional/verse/greensleeves.html* (accessed July 12, 2006).

"Gregorian Chant." Wikipedia. *http://en.wikipedia.org/wiki/Gregorian_chant* (accessed August 3, 2006).

Grimassi, Raven. *Ways of the Strega: Italian Witchcraft.* St. Paul, Minn.: Llewellyn Publications, 1995.

Halvorsen, Ingrid. "Stádhagaldr: Runic Yoga." Runes: Alphabet of Mystery, 1998–2004. *www.sunnyway.com/runes/stadha.html* (accessed July 31, 2006).

Hawker, Robert Stephen. "Aishah Shechinah." In *The Oxford Book of English Mystical Verse.* Edited by Nicholson and Lee. 1917, 81. *www.bartleby.com/236/81.html* (accessed June 23, 2006).

"Hey We to the Other World." 17th century. Index to Rounds. *www.personal.umich.edu/~msmiller/rcatch87.html* (accessed September 9, 2006).

Hill, Anne. "The Witch Song" in *Circle Round and Sing.* Sebastopol, Calif.: Serpentine Music Productions, 2000.

"History of Roman Catholic Novena." Roman Catholic Prayers. *www.roman-catholic-prayers.com/novena.html* (accessed September 26, 2006).

Holland, Eileen. *Holland's Grimoire of Magickal Correspondences: A Ritual Handbook.* Franklin Lakes, N.J.: New Page Books, 2005.

Jonson, Ben. "Hymn to Diana." In *The Oxford Book of English Verse: 1250–1900.* Edited by Arthur Quiller-Couch. 1919, 184. *www.bartleby.com/101/184.html* (accessed June 24, 2006).

K, Amber, and Azrael Arynn K. *Ritual Craft: Creating Rites for Transformation and Celebration*. St. Paul, Minn.: Llewellyn Publications, 2006.

Khalsa, Shakta Kaur. *Yoga for Women*. New York: DK, 2002.

Kipling, Rudyard. "The Elephant's Child." 1902. *www.online-literature.com/kipling/165/* (accessed July 31, 2006).

Legge, J. trans. "33." *Tao Te Ching (Sacred Books of the East, Vol. 39)*. 1891. *www.harvestfields.ca/ebook/01/014/00.htm* (accessed September 20, 2006).

Leland, Charles G. "To Diana." In *Aradia: Gospel of the Witches*, by Charles G. Leland. 1890. Custer, Wash.: Phoenix Publishing, Inc., 1990.

Lott, Joanna. "Keepers of History." Research/Penn State, Vol. 23, Issue 22, May, 2002. *www.rps.psu.edu/0205/keepers.html* (accessed April 6, 2006).

Lynn, Mary. *Every Page Perfect: A Full-Size Writer's Manual for Manuscript Format and Submission Protocol*. Mary Lynn, 1987, 1995. Revised and Updated Edition, Laceyville, Pa.: Toad Hall Press, 1997.

Manwaring, Kevan. *The Bardic Handbook: The Complete Handbook for the Twenty-First Century Bard*. Somerset, UK: Gothic Image Publications, 2006.

Matthews, Washington. "The White House Prayer." In *Navajo Myths, Prayers, and Songs*. 1906. *www.harvestfields.ca/ebook/NativeTribal/07bk/nmp05.htm* (accessed September 25, 2006).

Mojay, Gabriel. *Aromatherapy for Healing the Spirit: Restoring Emotional and Mental Balance with Essential Oils*. Rochester, N.Y.: Healing Arts Press, 1997.

Monaghan, Patricia. *The New Book of Goddesses & Heroines*. St. Paul, Minn.: Llewellyn Publications, 2002.

Mooney, James. "The Milky Way." In *Myths of the Cherokee* from Nineteenth Annual Report of the Bureau of American Ethnology 1897–98, Part I, 1900. *www.sacred-texts.com/nam/cher/motc/motc011.htm* (accessed October 30, 2006).

Mulligan, Alice. "A Song of Freedom." In *Anthology of Irish Verse*. Edited by Padraic Colum. 1922, 139. *www.bartleby.com/250/139.html* (accessed July 4, 2006).

Myers, Jack, and Don C. Wukasch. *Dictionary of Poetic Terms*. Denton, Tex.: University of North Texas Press, 1985, 2003.

Nashe, Thomas. "Spring." In *The Oxford Book of English Verse: 1250-1900*. Edited by Arthur Quiller-Couch. 1919, 166. *www.bartleby.com/101/166.html* (accessed July 8, 2006).

Nuwer, Hank. *How to Write Like an Expert About Everything*. Cincinnati, Ohio: Writer's Digest Books, 1995.

Olcott, Frances Jenkins. "The Battle of the Wizards." In *Wonder Tales from Baltic Wizards*, by Frances Olcott Jenkins. 1928. *www.sacred-texts.com/neu/bw/bw05.htm* (accessed June 27, 2006).

Owens, David W. *The Gods of Man: A Small Dictionary of Pagan Gods and Goddesses*. Chicago: Eschaton Productions, Inc., 1994.

Pennick, Nigel. *The Sacred World of the Celts: An Illustrated Guide to Celtic Spirituality and Mythology*. Rochester, N.Y.: Inner Traditions International, 1997.

Pope, Alexander. *An Essay on Criticism*. Published anonymously, 1711. *poetry.eserver.org/essay-on-criticism.html* (accessed July 12, 2006).

"Prayer and Sacrifice." Illustrated History of the Roman Empire. *www.roman-empire.net/religion/sacrifice.html* (accessed September 25, 2006).

Raeburn, Jane, ed. *The Pagan's Muse*. New York: Kensington, 2003.

Randall. "Sample Pagan Rituals." The Cauldron: A Pagan Forum, 1998–2007. *www.ecauldron.com/ritualindex.php* (accessed January 30, 2007).

Rattana, Guru. "Mudras." Kundalini Yoga, 1999–2005. *www.kundaliniyoga.org/mudras.html* (accessed August 1, 2006).

RavenWolf, Silver. *To Light a Sacred Flame: Practical WitchCraft for the Millennium*. St. Paul, Minn.: Llewellyn Publications, 1999.

"Rhapsode." Wikipedia. *http://en.wikipedia.org/wiki/Rhapsode* (accessed February 12, 2006).

Richardson, Stephen Scott. *WPI Technical Theatre Handbook*. Worcester, Mass.: Worcester Polytechnic Institute, 1996. *www.gweep.net/~prefect/pubs/iqp/technical_theatre_handbook.pdf* (accessed November 17, 2006).

Roget, Peter. *Roget's Thesaurus of English Words and Phrases* (150th Anniversary E. Roget's Thesaurus edition). Edited by George W. Davidson. New York: Penguin Books Ltd., 2006.

Roget's Thesaurus Online. Lexico Publishing Group, LLC, 2006. *thesaurus.reference.com* (accessed October 7, 2006).

Ryan, Marah Ellis. "Hymn to Agni." In *Pagan Prayers*. 1913. *www.sacred-texts.com/pag/ppr/ppr21.htm* (accessed September 25, 2006).

———. "Hymn to the Unknown God." *www.sacred-texts.com/pag/ppr/ppr35.htm* (accessed September 30, 2006).

————. "Prayer of the Sower" *www.sacred-texts.com/pag/ppr/ ppr17.htm* (accessed October 6, 2006).

Sandburg, Carl. "Fog." In *Chicago Poems* by Carl Sandburg. New York: Henry Holt and Company, 1916. *http://poetry.eserver.org/ chicago-poems.txt* (accessed July 7, 2006).

Shakespeare, William. "Sonnet C." In *The Complete Works of William Shakespeare*. Edited by W.J. Craig. Oxford, UK: Oxford University Press, 1914. www.bartleby.com/70/50100.html (accessed July 20, 2006).

Sidney, Sir Philip. "Sleep." In *The Oxford Book of English Verse: 1250– 1900*. Edited by Arthur Quiller-Couch, 94. 1919. *www.bartleby.com/101/94.html* (accessed June 23, 2006).

"The Skald of the Scandinavian Medieaval Ages." *www.geocities.com/ athens/forum/1734/squirrel.htm#skald* (accessed April 6, 2006).

Skene, William F. "The Pleasant Things of Taliessin." In *The Book of Taliessin IV*, in *The Four Ancient Books of Wales*. Edited by William F. Skene. Edinburgh, UK: Edmonston and Douglas, 1868. *www.sacred-texts.com/neu/celt/fab/fab113.htm* (accessed July 23, 2006).

Spellwerx. "Number Correspondences." Spellwerx, 2001. *www.spelwerx.com/number_correspondences.html* (accessed September 20, 2006).

Spenser, Edmund. "Sonnet LXXV" of *Amoretti and Epithalamion*. In *English poetry I: from Chaucer to Gray*. Edited by Charles W. Eliot, New York: P.F. Collier & Son, 1909–14. *www.bartleby.com/40/ 81.html (accessed July 21, 2006)*.

Starhawk. *The Spiral Dance: A Rebirth of the Ancient Religion of the Goddess*. New York: Harper & Row, 1979. 20th Anniversary edition, San Francisco: HarperSanFrancisco, 1999.

Stevenson, Robert Louis. "Summer Sun." In *A Child's Garden of Verses and Underwoods* by Robert Louis Stevenson. New York: Current Literature Publishing Co., 1906.

Stone, Merlin. *When God Was a Woman*. New York: Dial Press, 1976.

Thoreau, Henry David. "Smoke." In *An American Anthology, 1787– 1900*. Edited by Edmund Clarence Stedman. Boston: Houghton Mifflin, 1900. *www.bartelby.com/248/302.html* (accessed July 12, 2006).

Toumanian, Haroutune. "Morning." In *Armenian Legends and Poems* by Zabelle C. Boyajian. (1916): 32. *www.sacred-texts.com/asia/alp/ alp29.htm#page_32* (accessed October 26, 2006).

Turner, Dr. Judy, Dr. Angela Taylor, and Dr. Kim Shahabudin. "How to Improve Your Memory." The University of Reading, January 12, 2007. *www.rdg.ac.uk/studyskills/study_resources/study_guides/memory.htm#Summary/Example_of_spidergram* (accessed January 30, 2007).

Valiente, Doreen. *Natural Magic*. Boston: St. Martins Press, 1975.

Weelkes, Thomas. "Strike It Up Tabor." In *Ayres of Phantasticke Spirites for Three Voices*. 1608. *www.cpdl.org/wiki/index.php/Strike_it_up_Tabor_%28Thomas_Weelkes%29* (accessed August 14, 2006).

West, Kate, and the Hearth of Hecate. "Merry Meet." In *Elements of Chants*. CD. Pyewacket Productions, 2004.

Wilde, Oscar. "Theocritus: a Villanelle." In *Poems* by Oscar Wilde. Boston: Robert Brothers, 1881. *www.bartleby.com/143/37.html* (accessed July 23, 2006).

Wilson, Catherine. "Poetry: The Forms and the History: Elegy." Prose-n-Poetry, December 20, 2002. *www.prose-n-poetry.com/display_work/7482* (accessed July 8, 2006).

Wilson, Terri. "A Cup of Creativi-tea: Brainstorming." Law Library Resource Xchange, LLC., September 17, 2006. *www.llrx.com/columns/creativitea6.htm* (accessed January 30, 2007).

Wolf, Susan Falkenrath, and Reclaiming. "Circle Casting Song" in *Second Chants*. CD. Sebastopol, Calif.: Serpentine Music Productions, 1994.

Wordsworth, William. "The World Is Too Much With Us." *The Complete Poetical Works*. Houndmills, UK: Macmillan and Co., 1888. *www.bartleby.com/145/ww317.html* (accessed July 20, 2006).

"Writers Guidelines Database." Writers Write, Inc., 1997–2007. *www.writerswrite.com/writersguidelines* (accessed December 4, 2006).

The Writing Center. "Brainstorming." University of North Carolina at Chapel Hill, 1998-2005. *www.unc.edu/depts/wcweb/handouts/brainstorming.html* (accessed January 30, 2007).

Yeats, W.B. "The Song of Wandering Aengus." In *The Wind Among the Reeds* by J. Lane. New York: The Bodley Head, 1899. *www.poetryconnection.net/poets/William_Butler_Yeats/1263* (accessed July 13, 2006).

"Yoga Chants." Yoga Insight. *www.yoga-insight.com/history/yoga-chants.aspx* (accessed August 14, 2006).

Zell-Ravenheart, Oberon, ed. *Grimoire for the Apprentice Wizard.* Franklin Lakes, N.J.: New Page Books, 2004.

Index

About the Author

Elizabeth Barrette works as a writer and editor, spanning nonfiction, fiction, and poetry. Her main fields include alternative religions, speculative fiction, and gender studies. She serves as managing editor of *PanGaia*. She is involved with establishing the Pagan Fiction Award sponsored by Blessed Bee, Inc. and Llewellyn Worldwide. In the Grey School of Wizardry, she is the dean of studies and professor of several departments.

Her work has earned recognition including poet laureate status at *Sol Magazine* and nomination for the Rhysling Award. She has published various articles and columns on poetry, nonfiction writing, and public speaking. Her spiritual articles and essays have appeared throughout the Pagan field. Publication credits include magazines *The Beltane Papers*, *CIRCLE Magazine*, *Green Egg*, *PagaNet News*, *PanGaia*, and *SageWoman*; the Llewellyn *Magickal Almanac*, *Spell-a-Day Almanac*, *Witches' Calendar*, *Witches' Datebook* and other annuals; plus poetry and articles in *Companion for the Apprentice Wizard*.

Elizabeth Barrette belongs to the Science Fiction Poetry Association. She supports small press and electronic publication through book reviews and public speaking. She often presents panels and workshops at science fiction conventions and Pagan festivals on such topics as writing nonfiction, composing poetry, and magical ethics. She lives in central Illinois, where her favorite pastimes include gardening for wildlife and studying obscure languages.

For more information on Elizabeth Barrette's writing, and on Pagan/magical writing in general, visit her LifeJournal at: *http://ysabetwordsmith.livejournal.com.*